SECOND WORLD WAR POEMS

Hugh Haughton is Emeritus Professor of Modern Literature at the University of York. He is author of *The Poetry of Derek Mahon* (2007) and editor of *The Chatto Book of Nonsense Poetry* (1988); *Sigmund Freud, The Uncanny* (2004); and, with Valerie Eliot, *The Letters of T. S. Eliot Volumes 1 and 2* (2008).

Second World War Poems

Chosen by HUGH HAUGHTON

faber

First published in 2004
by Faber & Faber Ltd
The Bindery, 51 Hatton Garden
London, ECIN 8HN
This paperback edition first published in 2023

Photoset by RefineCatch Ltd, Bungay, Suffolk
Printed and bound by CPI Group (UK) Ltd, Croydon, CRO 4YY

A CIP record for this book
is available from the British Library

ISBN 978-0-571-38260-6

10 9 8 7 6 5 4 3 2 1

Contents

[x]

[xiv]

Introduction

In the dark times
Will there be singing?
Yes, there will be singing
About the dark times.
  Bertolt Brecht

  It has to think about war
And it has to find what will suffice.
  Wallace Stevens, 'Of Modern Poetry'

I

I will sing/ of what the others never set eyes on
  Keith Douglas

In most people's minds 'war poetry' refers to the English poetry of the First World War, and the typical 'war poet' is Wilfred Owen or Siegfried Sassoon. In contrast, the poetry of the Second World War is much more shadowy. Indeed it has been largely overshadowed by that of the First. The names of Keith Douglas and Alun Lewis still figure as important poets of the 1939–45 war but their poems certainly don't circulate like Owen's, Rosenberg's or Edward Thomas's. The Second World War and Holocaust still loom large in our amnesiac culture, figuring prolifically in films, television documentaries, history books and fiction. In contrast, the poetry of the Second World War is almost a dead letter. It has nothing like the same currency as that of the First. This is strange for many reasons, not least because the best poetry written during and about the 1939–45 War is as powerful and compelling as anything written about the previous war. This is true of poetry in English, but even more so if we take account of poetry in other languages.

Paradoxically the main obstacle to the recognition of the force and variety of the poetry of World War II in English has been the myth of the 'war poet' forged during and after World War I. The myth was hammered out in poems by Wilfred Owen, Rosenberg and Sassoon and in memoirs such as Graves's *Goodbye to All That* (1929) and Sassoon's *Complete Memoirs of George Sherston* (1936), and it enjoyed wide currency before the Second World War, just as it does now. Robert Graves, writing in 1942 to explain the apparent absence of successful war poetry of World War II, observed that 'war poet' and 'war poetry' were 'terms first used in World War I and perhaps peculiar to it'.[1] Prior to then, he wrote, there had been 'patriotic verse and poems written in time of war, and even occasional poems written by soldiers on campaign', but no 'war poems in the now accepted sense'. In Graves's view, the 'boom for war poetry' was initially an idealistic extension of Georgian poetry on a patriotic front, and then a disillusioned reaction against it by those like Owen who suffered from shell-shock and broke down in the face of the horrors of the trenches. He went on to argue that the passing of the Conscription Act a few months before World War II 'made volunteer pride irrelevant and war poetry superfluous as a stimulus to recruiting'. The contemporary army was different too; no longer 'the amateur, desperate, happy-go-lucky, ragtime, lousy army of World War I', it was increasingly under the command of professional soldiers and increasingly 'mechanised'. As a result he thought the average soldier was probably living a safer and more boring life than 'his Aunt Fanny, the fire-watcher'. Though many would question Graves's generalisations, few would question his clinching argument. Unlike the First War poet, he says, 'it is extremely unlikely' his Second World War counterpart 'will have any qualms about the justice of the British cause or about the necessity of the war's continuance'. Herbert Read, another survivor from the earlier war, confirmed this. In 'To a Conscript of 1940', he voiced the disillusion of his generation about the First War ('We think we gave in vain. The world was not renewed'), but still urged his successor to fight, 'Knowing that there is no reward'. Rather than seeking to persuade the young conscript not to fight, he enjoined soldiers to go to battle in the conviction that 'To fight without hope is to fight with grace'.

Other British and American poets of World War II may not have shared Read's or Graves's views, but their ideas about war and poetry were largely shaped by the poets of their generation. 'Never such innocence again' as Philip Larkin wrote in 'MCMXIV'. Few in 1939 went to battle with the idealism of the young Rupert Brooke in 1914. Their literary education had been in the school of Eliot and Auden, not that of the English Georgians, and their historical education had taken place in the highly politicised culture of the 1930s. Soldier poets like Roy Fuller or Alan Ross would speak of their war-time experiences in the language of Auden or MacNeice, not that of De La Mare or Brooke. Asked what he wanted for Christmas in 1944, not long before his death in France, Keith Douglas replied, 'Baudelaire and cigarettes.'

Like Graves, the poets of the later conflict were acutely aware of the legacy of the First War poets, and initially unsure whether they were doomed to repeat them. Consciousness of this prompted C. Day Lewis to write 'Where are the War Poets?', Alun Lewis to address Edward Thomas in 'All Day it has Rained', and Keith Douglas to address 'Desert Flowers' to Isaac Rosenberg. 'Living in a wide landscape are the flowers', Douglas begins, before stepping back to acknowledge his predecessor, 'Rosenberg I only repeat what you were saying'. Nevertheless, Douglas's poem, while recognising the influence of the First World War poet, asserts an urge to do something different:

I see men as trees suffering
or confound the detail and the horizon.
Lay the coin on my tongue and I will sing
of what the others never set eyes on.

Douglas's poem lays claim to a new currency, a kind of posthumous authority, but also records the sheer difficulty of writing – and seeing clearly – in the midst of his mental confusion where it is hard to distinguish between men suffering and trees, between the detail and the horizon. Donald Bain acknowledges a comparable problem in his 'War Poet': 'We in our haste can only see the small components of the scene/ We cannot tell what incidents will focus on the final screen.' Unlike Owen and Sassoon, Bain says, 'We do not wish to moralise, only to ease our dusty throats.' Given that most poets believed in the battle against Nazism, the sheer propaganda force of poems such as 'Dulce et Decorum Est' was irrelevant to most in the armed services. Despite that, the need for the poet to somehow record and witness the reality of war persisted. In 'Poem in 1944', for example, Robert Conquest wrote 'I cannot write the poem of war/ Neither the colossal dying nor the local scene', but confessed that he had to believe 'That somewhere the poet is working who can handle/ The flung world and his own heart', offering him as material 'the debris/ Of five years undirected storm in self and Europe'.

The five years of undirected storm produced an extraordinary harvest of poems, many of which gain their impact from their documentation of the 'local scene'. More than that, however, the primary experience one finds in poem after poem is a sense of dislocation, ruination. In that sense, the Second

World War – with the Holocaust and global refugee crisis it brought with it – represented a challenge to the poetic imagination comparable to, or greater than, the First. Exiled in Svenborg on the eve of the War, the German poet Brecht said that he followed the struggle, and sent his friends poems which were 'frightened into existence/ By deadly visions across/ Sound and foliage'. It was there he wrote the words about 'singing/ About the dark times' I have used as an epigraph.

2

The kind of war is chang'd
    Herbert Read, 'War and Peace'

We are filthy with war and Orpheus swarms with insects
    Salvatore Quasimodo, 'Dialogue'

The Second World War was a very different war to the First. Political transformation in Europe and the Far East, as well as major developments in the technology and strategy of warfare, changed the scale and nature of the conflict. The triumph of modernism in the cultural sphere had modified the situation of the poet, but so did the rise of Fascism in Germany, Stalinism in Russia, the politicisation of literature in the 1930s, the Spanish Civil War. The Second World War in Europe was triggered by the rise of Nazism in Germany and the threat posed by Hitler's expansionist militarism. The 'dark times' Brecht talked of were times of ideological alliances and conflicts on many fronts, with battles and alliances between nations mapped out against the battles and alliances between Fascism, Communism and Democracy. The scale, location and technology of the Second World War also made it a completely different kind of war. Rather than being fought in a relatively confined theatre, as the First World War was, it was genuinely global. Technological developments in bomb-making, tanks, planes and weapons of mass destruction meant this was a war which affected the civilian population as much as the military, cities and citizens as much as the armed forces.

It is hard now to grasp the sheer scale and intensity of the Second World War, or the havoc it wrought across the face of the world. Historians calculate that something like 85 million young men and women world-wide were engaged as combatants in armies, navies and air-forces during the course of the conflict, including 12 million in both the Soviet Union and the USA, 10 million in Germany, 6 million in Japan, and 4.5 million in Britain and Italy. Seventeen million of them were killed. In the Battle of Kursk alone, fought in the USSR in 1943, there were two million men engaged in combat. According to Joanna Bourke, 'the dedication of the entire globe to the waging of war and the breaking down of distinctions between the battlefield and the home front were the chief traits of this conflict'.[2] 'Without question', she observed, 'the Second World War propelled the notion of "total war" into dizzily horrifying heights.' She points out that where twenty-eight states took part in World War I, 'sixty-one states leapt at each other's throats between 1939 and 1945', and 'while only 5 per cent of deaths in the 1914–18 war were civilian deaths, 66 per cent of deaths in the 1939–45 war were of civilians'. Paul Fussell makes a similar point when he said that 'if the battle of the Somme constitutes a scandal because 20,000 British soldiers were killed in one day, twice that number of civilians were asphyxiated and burned to death in the bombing of Hamburg. Seventy thousand died at Hiroshima, 35,000 at Nagasaki, and the same at Dresden. Among British bomber crews, over 55,000 were killed, more than all the British officers killed and wounded in the First World War.'[3] In a single raid on Tokyo in 1945 83,000 people were killed (which was incidentally 20,000 more than all the British deaths from air attack throughout the war). During the course of the war as a whole over 78 million people were killed or wounded, including the 6 million Jews massacred by the Nazis, but also the 14–16 million non-Jews who were also the victims of Nazi mass murder. In his *Second World War: An Illustrated History*, A. J. P. Taylor observed that 'in contrast to previous wars of modern times, more civilians were killed than soldiers – some by aerial bombardment, others murdered by the Germans as partisans or hostages, many more murdered gratuitously in execution of Nazi racial doctrine, many perishing from hardship and starvation while carrying out forced labour in Germany or when besieged at Leningrad and elsewhere.'[4] For example, 5.8 million Polish civilians were murdered by the Germans, a third of them Jews. Soviet Russia lost 10 per cent of her population: 6 million soldiers killed, and 14 million soldiers and civilians murdered by the Germans. Four and a half million Germans were killed in battle, three-quarters of them on the Eastern Front; 593,000 German civilians were killed in air bombardment. Japan lost over a million combatants in battle and 600,000 civilians from air bombardment. Between 3 and 13 million people died in China, more from general hardship than actual fighting. Out of Europe's 9 million Jews, between 5 and 6 million were murdered by the Germans in the gas chambers. The Gypsies of Eastern Europe were virtually exterminated by the same means.

After Hiroshima, after Nuremberg, after the revelation of the systematic genocide of the Jews of Europe, after Stalingrad and Dunkirk, after the mass return of millions of soldiers to traumatised or shattered homelands in 1945, after the final casualty figures, the sheer scale of the carnage and disruption suffered by entire populations constituted an unprecedented challenge to the imagination. Joanna Bourke calculates that around 55 million people were dead, with on average 20,000 killed each day of the war. A high proportion of these were children, and 13 million children were without parents at the end of the war. By the close of the war, as Joanna Bourke puts it, 'hundreds of millions of people were forced to sift through the ashes of their ruined lives'.[5] In Europe as a whole, 50 million people had been driven from their homes. The material destruction of cities and industrial resources was equally devastating. Russia lost 6 million houses and 31,850 factories, the Germans lost 2.5 million houses, with Hamburg suffering more than the whole of Great Britain, and in France resources were effectively halved as a result of German destruction and Allied bombardment. Most Japanese cities were in ruins, while in Britain half a million homes were destroyed and 4 million damaged. Mass destruction of cities was the grim complement of the mass murder of millions of human beings.

The scale of ruin brought about by the war beggars representation. Towards the end of the First World War, Wilfred Owen declared not only that 'the poetry is in the pity' but that 'all a poet can do today is warn'. In the aftermath of the Second World War, the German philosopher Theodor Adorno argued that 'to write poetry after Auschwitz is barbaric'.[6] Fortunately, poets felt otherwise. The Second World War may have smashed many things and called into question fundamental assumptions about human culture, but its impact on poetry in English and other languages was not only negative. It might be argued that 'war poetry', as written by Owen, was one of the many casualties of this Second War, but that the war entered into and was represented in poetry in many other ways. 'The dance of poetry came to an end', Tadeusz Różewicz wrote, 'in concentration camps created by totalitarian systems.'[7] The dance, not lyric poetry itself. The American war correspondent Martha Gellhorn, witness of seven wars, including World War II, wrote in 1959, 'When I was not being a witness, I read the testimony of other witnesses and imagined distant wars.' Her endlessly repeated message, she said, was that 'War happens to people one by one'.[8] The best poems of the Second World War, though as formally different from Gellhorn's reports as they could be, remind us of the same truth. Poetry is instantiation, and these poems offer individual reports of local details that flare up and throw light on the immense and unimaginable theatre of the war. In his essay on 'Poetry and Ruins', the Polish poet Czeslaw Mil´osz argued that poetry in Polish was re-shaped amid the ruins, as in the abrasive fragmentary anti-lyrics of his contemporary, Tadeusz Róz˙ewicz. This is not true of English or American poetry in the same way. Not only did the armed forces throw up poets such as Keith Douglas, Randall Jarrell and Hamish Henderson, but the war became a central historical force in some of the major poetic monuments of the period. These include Eliot's *Little Gidding*, Pound's *Pisan Cantos*, H.D.'s *Trilogy*, Auden's *New Year's Letter* and Wallace Stevens's 'Consideration of the Hero in Time of War'. If we open our eyes to it, the war, far from being the province only of soldier poets, looms persuasively in the poetry of the time. This anthology is an invitation to consideration of the poet in the time of the Second World War, and of the war seen through the lens of individual poems.

3

a theme/ Born out of the experience of war's horrible extreme
F. T. Prince, 'Soldiers Bathing'

> *You pick a fragment*
> *Of grenade which pierced the body of a song*
> Czeslaw Miłosz, 'A Book in the Ruins'

There have been numerous important anthologies of Second World War poetry. They embody different priorities and quite distinct notions of what and where the poetry of the Second War is: whether it is verse written by combatants in the armed forces, or poetry that happens to be written in war-time, or poetry explicitly about the war and its battles written by anyone for whom it is a subject. Beyond that, there is a question as to whether what is at stake is English-language poetry – taking in American, Canadian and Australian writers, as well as those from the British Isles – or something larger that takes into account non-Anglophone literatures. Whereas the canon of First World War poetry in English is relatively stable, that of the Second World War is still an open question. The present anthology tries to address that open question and show something of the variety of contemporary poetic responses to what Joanna Bourke calls 'the greatest cataclysm in modern history'.

As noted earlier, C. Day Lewis published a notorious wartime poem called 'Where are the War Poets?' The answer ironically was 'All around you'. Editors had already begun to launch anthologies of war poetry soon after the war got under way. This resulted in books such as *Poems from the Forces* and *Poets of this War* as well as *Oasis*, an extraordinary literary magazine produced by British forces in North Africa, and Tambimuttu's *Poetry in Wartime*, produced by Poetry London. Reviewing Tambimuttu's book, a critic in *The Listener* said, 'most wartime anthologies of poetry will survive, if they survive at all, merely as historical or sociological documents'. Though he thought *Poetry in Wartime* a 'brilliant exception', this is true of most of the wartime anthologies, whether they drew exclusively on the work of poets on active service, like *Poems from the Forces*, or on contemporary writers writing about war, like Poetry in Wartime. A second wave of anthologies was launched in the 1960s, operating with the benefit of hindsight but still generally confining themselves to English and American poets in the armed forces. These include Ian Hamilton's *Poetry of War* (1966), Brian Gardner's *Terrible Rain* (1966) and Charles Hamblett's *I Burn for England: An Anthology of the Poetry of World War II* (1966). These are valuable, thematically organised anthologies of verse from the time, with Ian Hamilton's the most narrowly literary in its orientation and Gardner's the most documentary. They were followed by *Return to Oasis*, a dazzling document of the poetry written by British poets in just one of the theatres of war, and Victor Selwyn's more wide-ranging anthology, *The Voice of War: Poems of the Second World War* (1996), drawing on work by members of the British forces more generally, arranged thematically in terms of the different theatres of operation. A corrective to the overwhelmingly masculine constitution of these books was provided by Catherine Reilly's *Chaos of the Night: Women's Poetry and Verse of the Second World War* (1984) and Anne Powell's *Shadows of War* (1999). A different corrective view of the literary legacy of the War was offered by two pioneering international anthologies, Daniel Weissbort's *The Poetry of Survival: Post-War Poets of Central and Eastern Europe* (1991) and Desmond Graham's *Poetry of the Second World War: An International Anthology* (1995). They remind us that all the major contemporary poets of Russia and Eastern and Western Europe wrote important poetry about the war, and show the ways it shaped literature in all the war-torn and occupied countries of Europe and beyond.

This personal anthology is indebted to all its predecessors. Like them, however, it invites us to rethink our conceptions of and canons of poetry about war. Most selections of World War II verse are built around the 'war poetry' of combatants, soldiers who wrote or poets who served in the forces. This one draws on such poets, but casts the net more widely. It recruits poems by poets who fought in the Allied and other forces but also poems by others: civilians, women, prisoners of war, refugees, victims of the Holocaust, and people of many nationalities. This was not a war confined to the battlefield or to one continent. Events like the Blitz, the mass bombing of cities, the German occupation of France, Holland and most of Europe, the Holocaust and the atomic bomb, dissolved the difference between the 'battlefield' and everywhere else. This was a war that directly affected the whole population of countries across Europe, Russia, the Middle East and Far East, and a catastrophe for civilians as well as soldiers. Following in the footsteps of Desmond Graham, the anthology samples the range of verse by those outside the armed forces and – by way of translation – beyond the confines of the English language. It draws exclusively on writers who lived through the war, and mainly on poetry written during the war or in its immediate aftermath, though I have also included a handful of poems by later poets with childhood memories of war-time (Roy Fisher, Tony Harrison, Derek Mahon, Geoffrey Hill).

Any anthology is a patchwork, but this is an international patchwork. It seeks by a scatter of instances to capture the ways the war entered poetry and transformed it in many countries. Though biased towards poetry in English, it sets English-language poets such as Keith Douglas, Hamish Henderson and Randall Jarrell within a larger frame. Major poets in many languages wrote about the war and took their later bearings from it. These include the Russian poets Anna Akhmatova and Boris Pasternak, the German poets Bertolt Brecht, Paul Celan and Nelly Sachs, the Polish poets Czeslaw Miłosz, Tadeusz Różewicz, Zbigniew Herbert and Aleksander Wat, the French poets Louis Aragon, Paul Eluard, René Char and

Robert Desnos, the Italian poets Primo Levi, Salvatore Quasimodo and Montale, the Czech poet Miroslav Holub, the Hungarian poets Miklós Radnóti, János Pilinsky and Ágnes Gergely, and others. My aim has been to include powerful, distinctive and various poems that respond, directly or indirectly, to the challenge of the Second World War and to their medium. Though some of the finest English-language poems of the war made use of the hardened armour of traditional form – I think of Richard Wilbur's 'Snow in Alsace', Yvor Winters' 'To a Military Rifle, 1942' – many of the poems from Europe were compelled to break new poetic ground. Perhaps because the carnage and devastation were on a scale far beyond that experienced by English or Americans, for many it was as if the whole language of poetry had to be broken down and reinvented. Poets such as Paul Celan, Różewicz and Herbert give the lie to Adorno's claim that after Auschwitz, lyric poetry was impossible. Certain kinds of poetry were henceforth impossible but the horrors of the war shocked lyric poetry into a different formal reality. 'I shall never go back to the old forms', Keith Douglas wrote. The Eclogues of Miklós Radnóti, Anna Akhmatova's 'Wind of War', Brecht's Svenborg poems and Paul Celan's *Deathfugue* are major modern lyrics that in Stevens's words, both 'speak about war' and seek, against all odds, to articulate 'what will suffice'.

Though the anthology looks beyond Britain and beyond 'war poetry' as defined by the First World War, it includes the work of soldier poets who bear witness to the realities of battle in the deserts of North Africa, in the forests of Burma, in ships on the Atlantic, in bombers over Europe and elsewhere. These include English poets like Keith Douglas, Welsh poets like Alun Lewis, Scottish poets like Sorley Maclean and Hamish Henderson as well as American poets like Randall Jarrell and Richard Eberhart. However, other kinds of poets grappled with the realities and horrors of the war in other ways and other places, and I have tried to represent this too. The scale of ruination was unprecedented, affecting the whole fabric of daily life across much of the world. In 'Ruins and Poetry', published in *The Witness of Poetry*, the great Polish poet Czeslaw Miłosz argued that it was the encounter with the 'hell of the twentieth century' during the years 1939–45 that gave modern Polish poetry its distinctive character. He noted that in the war years 'poetry was the main genre of underground literature', being circulated in manuscript or clandestine publications, eventually resulting in the publication of Poetry of Fighting Poland in 1972, with 1,912 pages of poems and songs written mostly during the German occupation. For Miłosz, much of this is primarily of 'documentary' value rather than as poetic witness, and it was not until after the war that drastically new ways of writing and representing the reality of the war and its aftermath emerged. The same might be said of poetry elsewhere. For this reason, this anthology not only draws its nets wider than any one country or language but beyond the period of the war itself. The literature of the Holocaust, by definition, post-dated it. The Italian Holocaust poems of Primo Levi, like his uniquely compelling prose memoirs of the experience of the camps and post-war 'liberation', were necessarily retrospective – like the German language poems of Paul Celan and Nelly Sachs. It seemed to me essential to extend the compositional time-frame beyond the period of the war itself in order to demonstrate the struggle to represent its realities in poetry.

The cover shows a picture of a boy among the ruins of London in the Blitz. It is an image of both ruination and a kind of heroism, of catastrophic destruction on the one hand, and of the survival of reading on the other. In the rubble of the city, surrounded by the debris of the bombed bookshop, the readers go on reading. The image of the bombed city, alongside that of the concentration camp, is the archetypal icon of the Second World War. If these are the equivalents of the ruin-strewn, mud-sodden military landscapes of the Somme in the earlier war, they also assert what was different. Richard Eberhart wrote a poem called 'The Fury of Aerial Bombardment', and the devastation of major cities across the world – Berlin, Caen, Stalingrad, Hiroshima, London – was one of the most atrocious consequences and enduring images of the war. As noted earlier, Czeslaw Miłosz wrote an essay entitled 'Ruins and Poetry', and a sense of ruination at the heart of civilisation is crucial to much of the best poetry of the war, as is the idea of continuing, against all the odds, to read and write amid the ruins. In 1942 Miłosz wrote a poem called 'A Book in the Ruins' in which, in a 'world gone up in smoke', a reader picks up a book. Though 'legibility is disturbed', and a fragment of a grenade has 'pierced the body of a song', the 'world seems to drift from these pages/ Like the mist clearing on a field at dawn'. The reader still reads, but reads differently. And the poet still writes, though in ways and forms that register ruination.

4

I see no reason to be either musical or sonorous about things at present. When I do, I shall be so again, and glad to. I suppose I reflect the cynicism and the careful absence of expectation (it is not quite the same thing as apathy) with which I view the world. As many others to whom I have spoken, not only civilians and British soldiers, but Germans and Italians, are in the same state of mind, it is a true reflection. I never tried to write about war (that is battles and things, not London can Take it) . . . until I

had experienced it. Now I will write of it, and perhaps one day
cynic and lyric will meet and make me a balanced style.
  Keith Douglas, letter to J. C. Hall, Palestine, 1943

Everything that lies in rubble
reaches tenderly at me
  Aleksander Wat, 'To a Roman, my Friend'

Ted Hughes wrote in 1964 that the First World War was a national ghost that kept getting stronger, and the same might be said of the Second World War. The scale, intensity and extent of the ravage it wrought on global history remains a challenge to the poet as to the novelist, film-maker and historian. From the 1960s onwards, poets and anthologists took the war as their subject, creating a new wave of Second World War as well as First World War poetry. In recent poetry from the British Isles, Geoffrey Hill has made the legacy of the war a life-long preoccupation, from 'Requiem for the Jews of Europe' through 'September Song' and 'Ovid in the Third Reich' to *The Triumph of Love*; James Fenton's *Berlin Requiem* is his most compelling single work and Tom Paulin's *The Invasion Handbook* was to be the first of a projected sequence of works devoted to the war. The Second World War has shaped the modern world more than any other single event, and it continues to impact on modern literature, poetry included. Though I have selected a few poems about war-time childhoods by more recent poets, the anthology has not space to represent the ongoing engagement with the legacy of the war in modern poetry. Instead it seeks to demonstrate the importance of that encounter with 'the twentieth-century hell' of World War II for poetry in many languages, and represent the currency of poets like Celan, Akhmatova, Pilinsky and Różewicz in our own. Like translations from French earlier in the modern period, translations from Polish, Russian and

Hungarian poets have had a huge impact on post-war Anglophone poetry.

The poems have been chosen because they work as poems. War poetry is no exception to the principle that the best poems are written by the best poets. The anthology is therefore tilted towards the work of poets who wrote about war rather than that of participants in the war who also wrote poetry (the *Oasis* anthologies and others superbly represent these). I have chosen the poems for their continuing poetic force and arranged them alphabetically by the names of the poets, rather than thematically according to subject or geographically according to places or languages of origin. The kaleidoscope of individual poems has been accordingly shuffled into a sequence determined by authorial names, starting with the little-known English poet Valentine Ackland and the great Russian Anna Akhmatova, and ending with the distinguished Australian poet Judith Wright followed by the less-known Japanese poet Ei Yamaguchi. These are all poems inflected by history and I have included brief biographical notes at the back of the book, giving some information about the poets' places of origin, nationality, career and relationship to the war. Though minimal and hopefully unintrusive, the notes are designed as sign-posts to help situate the kaleidoscope of poems and poets in specific contexts. Where appropriate they also contain relevant information about the poems, as I have sought to avoid footnotes within the main body of the anthology.

I initially sought to differentiate poems written in English from translated work by putting them in different sections, but the distinction between 'national' and 'foreign', familiar and alien, 'us' and 'them', is everywhere under pressure in the poetry itself. In their splintered, individual ways, the poems chronicle the scale and nature of the six-year conflict in many places. There are poems here about the war in the desert, the air, the jungle and the sea. There are poems by soldiers, sailors, airmen and civilians. There are poems by men and women, and those who experienced the war as children as well as adults. There are poems about the Blitz, the bombing of cities, the prison camps, about exile and refugees, about the Holocaust and Hiroshima. There are poems about peace in war, the memory of war in peace, and the aftermath of war. As Alice Coats wrote in 'The Monstrous Regiment', however, 'war lends a spurious value to the male' and there are fewer poems by women than I would have liked. There are, however, poems by great English-language women poets, such as Elizabeth Bishop's war-time 'Roosters' and Marianne Moore's 'In Distrust of Merits', the first canto of H.D.'s *The Walls Do Not Fall*, E. J. Scovell's 'Daylight Alert', a documentary lyric alert to the shadow of war falling across a peaceful English city, and some characteristically spiky squibs by Stevie Smith. Many women poets in other languages wrote more directly of the devastation, and some of their voices can be heard in translation, including the Russian poet Anna Akhmatova, the German Jewish poet Nelly Sachs, the Polish poet Anna Swirszczyńska, the Hungarian Ágnes Nemes Nagy and the émigré Yiddish poet Rachel Korn.

Several major poets of the Second World War wrote from the heart of it, either as combatants, observers or participants. In English Keith Douglas, Hamish Henderson, Alun Lewis and Randall Jarrell wrote 'combatant' verse that measures up to the most enduring poems of the first war. Keith Douglas, Sorley Maclean and Henderson report from the war fought out in the North African desert in jaggedly articulated verse that captures the unprecedented nature of the battle theatre, fought by Europeans over African sand, rather than in the mud of the Somme, and with tanks rather than in trenches. It is also alive to the new conditions of writing, in the wake of 'First World War Poetry' and literary modernism. Randall Jarrell's still undervalued and neglected war-time poems report on the experience of American bombers, the bombed cities of Europe, refugees, Jews at Haifa, in ways which respond both to the pressures on the medium in the middle years of the century (and no one was better informed than the critic Jarrell about modern poetry) and to the new horrors of war. The Objectivist poet George Oppen, though poetically silent during the war and immediately afterwards, returned to his army experiences in later poems, including the compellingly estranged 'Myth of the Blaze', based on his experience hiding in a 'fox-hole' during the American landings in France in 1944, a dazzling poem which has nothing in common with 'war poetry' as usually conceived. The anthology sets these alongside civilian poems by the surviving modernists Eliot, Pound, Stevens and H.D. as well as by the 30s poets W. H. Auden – a major civilian war poet like Brecht – and Louis MacNeice. The map of English-speaking verse includes work by English and American poets but also Scots poets (including Garioch, Montgomerie, Maclean and Henderson), the Welsh Alun Lewis and Dylan Thomas, the Irish Louis MacNeice and W. R. Rodgers, and the Australians Kenneth Slessor and John Manifold.

The war was inevitably experienced very differently in different countries and the poetry of the war is comparably various. The Anglophone countries of Britain and the USA escaped invasion and occupation. Elsewhere, poets experienced the horrors of inv-asion, occupation, exile and the concentration camps. War poetry in France, for example, largely took the form of 'Resistance Poetry'. Ian Higgins remarks that a 'remarkable feature' of the war in France was 'the sudden popularity of poetry', not only illegally produced

Resistance poetry during the Nazi occupation but *'contrebande'* poetry that was legally published but cryptically subversive. Literary magazines like *Confluences* in Lyon, or *Poètes Casqués* edited by Pierre Seghers, were crucial focal points for the Resistance, while one of the most resounding *contrebande* volumes, *Domaine Français*, had to be published in Switzerland in 1943. It weighed in at 450 pages. Francis Ponge, a poet active inthe Resistance, wrote prolifically during wartime, including his extraordinary notes from a poet's laboratory, *Rage de L'Expression*, but his work deals with the war itself only in the most oblique, codified way. His elliptic eight-line poem 'La Métamorphose' (Metamorphosis) appeared in a Lyon Art Gallery that was also a local centre of the Resistance. It was written on a blackboard (for quick erasure in case of danger). This is a war poem, but so deeply coded that it is hard for us now to see it as such:

> You can twist the elastic of your heart
> Round the foot of the stalks
> But it's not as a caterpillar
> You will know the flowers
> When more than one sign announces
> Your rush towards happiness
>
> . . .
>
> He trembles and with a single leap
> Rejoins the butterflies.

This is certainly not the kind of poetry we would recognise in English as 'war poetry', yet it was apparently used as a recruitment poem as much as anything by Rupert Brooke. Its function was to get people to join the Resistance. The poetry of resistance is, in this respect, a very different species to anything in English. I have included poems by leading resistance poets such as Aragon, Éluard and Frénaud, though little survives translation from its original language and moment.

Comparable poetic and documentary testimony can be found in major poets across Europe who, whether as combatants or civilians, were caught up in the nightmarishly expanding zone of violence and dislocation. Some were soldiers, some prisoners, some witnesses of atrocity, many were refugees. Anna Akhmatova wrote her great masterpiece *Poem without a Hero* in 1942–3, intercutting shots of besieged war-time Leningrad with memories of the past. She also wrote 'In the Fortieth Year', two sonnets commemorating the fall of Paris and the bombing of London, and 'The Wind of War', a sequence about the Nazi invasion of Russia and Russian endurance, written in exile. Polish poets like Różewicz, Wat and Miłosz were caught in the eye of the storm and helped rebuild Polish poetry in the wake of the ruins. Różewicz with his stripped-down, hard-edged poems seemed almost to deconstruct the poetic itself. Of the work of the Hungarian poet János Pilinsky, Ted Hughes, his translator, wrote that what he encountered in concentration camps 'was a revelation of the new man: humanity stripped of everything but the biological persistence of cells'. His was a voice speaking 'from the disaster-centre of the modern world'.[9] Miklós Radnóti was already a recognised Hungarian poet before the war, whose work bore the imprint of poetic modernism of many kinds. However, from 1940, when as a Jew he was conscripted into a Forced Labour Battalion, till he was shot on a forced march in 1944, he wrote a series of extraordinary poems, not only seeking to capture the horrors of his experience but to explore the limits of the poetic. In 1938, before the war, he had translated Virgil's ninth Eclogue for a planned *Pastoral Hungarian Virgil*, and during the grim years of the early 40s he wrote a series of elaborately staged war Eclogues in hexameters as well as a series of stark *Postcards* that translate his own and his culture's crisis into poetic form. When his body was exhumed in 1945, a notebook full of poems was recovered from his overcoat. Reproduced and translated as *Camp Notebook* by Francis Jones, and introduced by George Szirtes, this is one of the most moving testimonies to the survival of poetry in the Second World War.[10]

With Nazi Germany the prime mover in the war, and Nazism the agent of its greatest atrocities, the German poetry that survives is of exile and self-critique. Brecht, as a refugee from the Third Reich, wrote a series of powerful resistance poems of exile, elegy and protest, including the early '1940' (one of many poems from many places bearing the mark of particular dates in their title) and 'War has been Given a Bad Name', written after the end of the conflict. Taken together, they are comparable to anything written by the First War poets in England. Downbeat, minimal, sceptical and epigrammatic, these poems provided the makings of an idiom for post-war German poetry, East and West. German was also the language used by the Romanian and Jewish poet Paul Celan, who in 'Todesfuge' wrote a devastated and devastating requiem for the Jewish victims of Nazi genocide which has become what John Felstiner has called the 'benchmark for poetry "after Auschwitz" '. For Celan's friend Nelly Sachs, a German Jew exiled in Norway, the Holocaust was in some sense the premise of all her work, inspiring a minatory series of choric lamentations published in the wake of the war. Celan's poem asserts that 'Der Tod is ein meister aus Deutschland' ('death is a master from Germany'), and in the work of Celan and Sachs, we read poems painfully forged in the German of the 'master race' which are excruciatingly alive to the work of its literary *Meistern* but also seek a language to confront the horrors perpetrated by the Nazi regime. The Holocaust, of course, transcended national boundaries, and the Italian Primo Levi and the Israeli Dan Pagis, writing in Italian and Hebrew respectively, also published fragmented poems of witness born of their first-hand experience of the death camps. Levi's poems, like his memoir *If This is a Man*, are muted epitaphs and testimonies which seek to articulate the experience of survival.

Levi wrote a poem 'The Survivor', which begins 'Once more he sees his companions' faces' and ends 'It's not my fault if I live and breathe'. The Polish poet Różewicz wrote one with the same title. It begins and ends with the lines 'I am twenty-four/ led to slaughter/ I survived'. At its heart, however, is the memory of seeing 'truckfuls of chopped-up men/ who will not be saved' and the sense of moral vertigo war induced: 'Virtue and crime weigh the same/ I've seen it'. Much of the most compelling poetry of the war was produced in its aftermath by survivors and is, in a sense, *about* survival. It is written by people who needed to rebuild lives and re-imagine culture as well as find ways of rebuilding poetry in the wake of the 'crimes against humanity' embodied in the Holocaust, the bombings of Dresden and Hiroshima, and the physical and cultural devastation wrought by the world-wide conflict. This anthology is restricted to poets who were in some sense contemporary with and touched by the war, but not to poems written or published during war-time. Many of the most effective war poems, such as Auden's 'The Shield of Achilles', Brecht's 'War has been Given a Bad Name', Günter Eich's 'Inventory', Pilinsky's 'Frankfurt – 1945', Różewicz's 'Pigtail' or Zbigniew Herbert's 'The Rain' were written after the war, in the late 40s or early 50s. Louis Simpson recalls that it was on returning to Paris in 1948, after recovering from a nervous breakdown, that, as a result of a dream, he wrote out the poem 'Carentan O Carentan', a memory of his first time under fire, and then other poems in which he began 'piecing the war together'.[11] Other poems, such as Howard Nemerov's 'Redeployment', are about the obstinate persistence of a war that transformed the political landscape of Europe, in particular Eastern Europe, the Middle East (through the creation of the state of Israel in 1948) and the Far East.

Addressing the victims of the war at its end in 'Dedication' in his collection *Rescue* (1945), Czeslaw Miłosz wrote: 'What strengthened me, for you was lethal.'[12] At the end of the war, Samuel Beckett worked for a while with the Irish Red Cross at their makeshift hospital in Saint-Lô in Normandy. He wrote a miniscule poem called 'Saint-Lô' which makes no mention of the war but bears its mark. Saint-Lô had been bombed 'out of existence in one night', as Beckett noted in a piece entitled 'The Capital of the Ruins'. By the end of the war, many capitals were in ruins, but Saint-Lô is an unlikely capital. Beckett's piece speaks with the authority of first-person experience about his own take on ruination and reconstruction. It ends by invoking 'the possibility that some of those who were in Saint-Lô will come home realising that they got at least as good as they gave, that they got indeed what they could hardly give, a vision and sense of a time-honoured conception of humanity in ruins, and perhaps even an inkling of the terms in which our condition is to be thought again'.[13] The best poetry of the Second World War reports from comparable places in comparable terms. In another post-war poem, the great Polish poet Aleksander Wat noted that 'Everything that lies in rubble/ reaches tenderly at me:/ the ruins of my Warsaw/ the ruins of your Rome'. His poem ends with the image of two goats among the city ruins in April 1946, searching 'among remnants of glory/ for medicinal herbs'. They were foraging, he says, 'for earthly nourishment'.

1 Robert Graves, 'The Poets of World War II' (1942), *The Common Asphodel: Collected Essays on Poetry*, London: Hamish Hamilton, 1949, 307.

2 Joanna Bourke, *The Second World War: A People's History*, Oxford, 2001, 2.

3 Paul Fussell, *The Bloody Game: An Anthology of Modern War*, London and Sydney: Scribners, 1991, 307 ff.

4 A. J. P. Taylor, *The Second World War: An Illustrated History*, London: Penguin, 1985, 229.

5 Joanna Bourke, *The Second World War: A People's History*, Oxford, 2001, 214.

6 'Cultural Criticism and Society' (1951) trans. Samuel and Shierry Webster, in Brian O'Connor ed *The Adorno Reader*, Oxford: Blackwells, 2000, 196.

7 Quoted Adam Czerniawski, 'Introduction' to Tadeusz Różewicz, *Conversation with the Prince and other Poems* (1982), 13.

8 Martha Gellhorn, *The Face of War*, London: Granta Books, 1998.

9 Ted Hughes, 'Introduction', János Pilinsky, *Selected Poems* (1976) translated Ted Hughes and János Csokits, p. 9.

10 See Miklós Radnóti, *Camp Notebook* translated by Francis Jones, with an introduction by George Szirtes, Todmorden: Arc, 2000; *The Complete Poetry*, ed. and trans. Emergy George, Ann Arbor: Ardis, 1980; *Forced March: Selected Poems*, trans. Clive Wilmer and George Gömöri, Manchester: Carcanet, 1979.

11 In Ian Hamilton, *The Poetry of War 1939–45*, 172.

12 'Dedication', *Collected Poems 1931–87* (1988), 78.

13 Samuel Beckett, 'The Capital of the Ruins' (1946), *As the Story was Told*, London: Calder, 1990, 27–8.

SECOND WORLD WAR POEMS

7 October, 1940

One does not have to worry if we die:
Whoever dies, One does not have to bother
Because inside Her there is still another
And, that one wasted too, She yet replies
'Nothing can tire out Nature – here's another!'
   Fecundity par excellence is here,
   Lying in labour even on the bier.

Maternity's the holiest thing on earth
(No man who's prudent as well as wise
Concerns himself with what is in the skies);
Drain-deep below the slums another birth
   Sets angels singing – the other noise you hear
   May be the Warning, may be the All Clear.

Comfort ye My people! These reflections
Should help them die politely who must die,
And reconcile those left behind, who sigh
For loss of children or some near connections–
   Reflect! There is no need for grief nor gloom,
   Nature has ever another in Her womb.

Teeming and steaming hordes who helter-skelter
Stampede the city streets, to herd together
Angry and scared, in dark, in wintry weather–
Above ground still? Fear not, there's one deep shelter
   Open alike in Free and Fascist State,
   Vast, private, silent and inviolate.

Notes on Life at Home, February, 1942

What sounds fetched from far the wind carries tonight,
Do you hear them? Out where the sheep are
Huddled on wintry hill this cold night,
Under the lea of the hill folded;
There on the hard earth the wind goes
Massively over them, burdened with all that has colded
A thousand hearts, emptied a million hearts,
Slain twice and thrice a million. Over it blows
And like a flood pours into the house, under the doors,
Rushing like blood out of the dying veins, over the living it
    pours
And so, like a cunningly-channelled flood, empties away,
    departs
Leaving us dirtied with litter of not our own casualties, not
    our own hearts.

ANNA AKHMATOVA

In the Fortieth Year

I

When they come to bury the epoch,
Not with psalms will they mourn it,
But with nettles, with thistles,
They will have to adorn it.
And only the gravediggers jauntily
Work. Business won't wait!
And quietly, oh God, so quietly
That it is audible, is how time passes.
And afterwards it floats away
Like a corpse on a thawing river–
But the son won't recognise his mother,

*

And the grandson will turn away in anguish.
And heads will bow even lower
And the moon move like a pendulum.

And so it is – over ruined Paris
There is now such a silence.

August 5, 1940

2 TO THE LONDONERS

Time, with an impassive hand, is writing
The twenty-fourth drama of Shakespeare.
We, the celebrants at this terrible feast,
Would rather read *Hamlet, Caesar* or *Lear*
There by the leaden river;

We would rather, today, with torches and singing,
Be bearing the dove Juliet to her grave,
Would rather peer in at Macbeth's windows,
Trembling with the hired assassin—
Only not this, not this, not this,
This we don't have the strength to read!

1940

Translated from the Russian by Judith Hemschemeyer

The Wind of War

1 VOW

And she who is parting with her sweetheart today—
Let her forge her pain into strength.
By the children we swear, we swear by the graves,
That no one will force us to submit!

July 1941 Leningrad

2

Grandly they said good-bye to the girls,
Nonchalantly kissed Mother,
All dressed in brand-new clothes,
As if they were going to play soldier.

No bad, no good, no in-between . . .
They all took their place,
Where there is neither first, nor last . . .
They all lay down to sleep.

1943

And people's colorful daily round
Suddenly changed drastically.
But this was not a city sound,
Nor one heard in the villages.
It resembled a distant peal of thunder
As closely as one brother resembles another,
But in thunder there's the moisture
Of cool cloud towers
And the yearning of the meadows—
For the news of joyous showers.
But this was like scorching heat, dry,
And we didn't want to believe
The rumor we heard – because of
How it grew and multiplied,
Because of how indifferently
It brought death to my child.

September 1941

4

The birds of death are at the zenith.
Who will rescue Leningrad?

Be quiet – it is breathing,
It's still living, it hears everything:

How at the bottom of the Baltic Sea
Its sons groan in their sleep,

How from its depths come cries: 'Bread!'
That reach to the firmament . . .

But this solid earth is pitiless.
And staring from all the windows – death.

28 September 1941 (On the airplane)

5 COURAGE

We know what lies in balance at this moment,
And what is happening right now.
The hour for courage strikes upon our clocks,
And courage will not desert us.
We're not frightened by a hail of lead,
We're not bitter without a roof overhead–
And we will preserve you, Russian speech,
Mighty Russian word!
We will transmit you to our grandchildren
Free and pure and rescued from captivity
                    Forever!

23 February, 1942. Tashkent

6

Trenches have been dug in the garden,
No lights shine.
Peter's orphans,
Oh, my children!
It's hard to breathe underground,
Your temples throb,
Through the bombardment is heard
The voice of a child.

7

Knock with your little fist – I will open.
I always opened the door to you.

[8]

I am beyond the high mountain now,
Beyond the desert, beyond the wind and the heat,
But I will never abandon you . . .
I didn't hear your groans,
You never asked me for bread.
Bring me a twig from the maple tree
Or simply a little green grass,
As you did last spring.
Bring me in your cupped palms
Some of our cool, pure, Neva water,
And I will wash the bloody traces
From your golden hair.

23 April, 1942. Tashkent

8 NOX
(The statue 'Night' in the Summer Garden)

Little night!
Draped in stars,
In funereal poppies, with a sleepless owl . . .
Little daughter!
We hid you under
The garden's fresh dirt.
Empty now are the cups of Dionysus,
The gazes of love are stained with tears . . .
Passing over our city are
Your terrible sisters.

30 May, 1942

The Narvsky Gates were behind,
Ahead there was only death . . .
Thus the Soviet infantry marched
Straight into Big Bertha's blazing barrels.
They will write books about you:
'You laid down your life for your friends,'
Unpretentious lads–
Vankas, Vaskas, Alyoshkas, Grishkas–
Grandsons, brothers, sons!

29 February, 1944. Tashkent.

10

And you, my friends from the latest call-up!
My life has been spared to mourn for you.
Not to freeze over your memory as a weeping willow,
But to shout all your names to the whole wide world!
But never mind names!
      None of that matters – You are with us!
Everyone down on your knees!
      A crimson light pours!
And the Leningraders come through the smoke in even
  rows–
The living and the dead: for glory never dies.

August 1942. Dyurmen

11

To the right the vacant lots unfurl,
There's a strip of dawn as ancient as the world.

To the left, streetlights like gallows trees,
One, two, three . . .

And over everything a jackdaw's cry
And the moon's pallid face
Arise completely irrelevantly.

It's – not from this life and not from that one,
It's – when the golden age will dawn,

It's – when the war is over,
It's – when we meet once more.

29 April 1944. Tashkent

12

Something glorious is beginning gloriously,
With a thunderous crash, in snowy clouds,
Where the immaculate body of the land languishes,
Defiled by the enemy.
From there our native birches are stretching out
        their branches
To us, and waiting, and calling out to us,
And mighty Father Frosts
Are marching in formation with us.

January 1942

13

The first lighthouse flashed over the jetty,
The precursor of many–
And the sailor who had sailed seas packed with death,
Alongside death and on the way to death,
Took off his cap and wept.

14

Victory is standing at our door . . .
How shall we greet this guest we have yearned for?
Let women raise their children higher,
Children saved a thousand thousand times from death–
Thus will we respond to our long-awaited guest.

1942–1945

15 JANUARY 27, 1944

And on this starless January night,
Amazed at its fantastic fate,
Returned from the bottomless depths of death,
Leningrad salutes itself.

16 LIBERATION

A clean wind rocks the firs,
Clean snow covers the ground.
No longer hearing the tread of the enemy,
It rests, my land.

February 1945

Translated by Judith Hemschemeyer

LOUIS ARAGON

The Lilacs and the Roses

O months of blossoming, months of transfigurations,
May without a cloud and June stabbed to the heart,
I shall not ever forget the lilacs or the roses
Nor those the Spring has kept folded away apart.

I shall not ever forget the tragic sleight-of-hand,
The cavalcade, the cries, the crowd, the sun,
The lorries loaded with love, the Belgian gifts,
The road humming with bees, the atmosphere that spun,
The feckless triumphing before the battle,
The scarlet blood the scarlet kiss bespoke
And those about to die bolt upright in the turrets
Smothered in lilac by a drunken folk.

I shall not ever forget the flower-gardens of France—
Illuminated scrolls from eras more than spent—
Nor forget the trouble of dusk, the sphinx-like silence,
The roses all along the way we went;
Flowers that gave the lie to the soldiers passing
On wings of fear, a fear importunate as a breeze,
And gave the lie to the lunatic push-bikes and the ironic
Guns and the sorry rig of the refugees.

But what I do not know is why this whirl
Of memories always comes to the same point and drops
At Sainte-Marthe . . . a general . . . a black pattern . . .
A Norman villa where the forest stops;
All is quiet here, the enemy rests in the night
And Paris has surrendered, so we have just heard—

I shall never forget the lilacs nor the roses
Nor those two loves whose loss we have incurred:

Bouquets of the first day, lilacs, Flanders lilacs,
Soft cheeks of shadow rouged by death – and you,
Bouquets of the Retreat, delicate roses, tinted
Like far-off conflagrations: roses of Anjou.

Translated from the French by Louis MacNeice

Tapestry of the Great Fear

This landscape, masterpiece of modern terror
Has sharks and sirens, flying fish and swordfish
And hydra-headed birds like Lerna's hydra
What are they writing, white on blue, in the sky?
Skimmers of earth, steel birds that stitch the air
To the stone houses, strident comet-birds
Enormous wasps like acrobatic matchsticks
That deck the flaming walls with primroses
Or flights of pink flamingos in the sun
Kermess in Flanders, witches at their Sabbath
On a broomstick the Messerschmitt rides down
Darkness at noon, night of the new Walpurgis
Apocalyptic time. Space where fear passes
With all its baggage train of tears and trembling
Do you recognise the fields, the birds of prey?
The steeple where the bells will never ring
The farm carts draped with bedclothes. A tame bear
A shawl. A dead man dropped like an old shoe
Hands clutching the torn belly. A grandfather's clock
Roaming herds of cattle, carcasses, cries
Art bronzes by the roadside. Where will you sleep?

Children perched on the shoulders of strange men
Tramping off somewhere, while the gold of the barns
Gleams in their hair. Ditches where terror sits
The dying man in a cart who keeps asking
For herb tea, and complains of a cold sweat
A hunchbacked woman with a wedding dress
A birdcage that passed safely through the flames
A sewing machine. An old man. I can't walk
Just a step more. No, let me die here, Marie
Evening soars down with silent wingbeats, joining
A velvet Breughel to this Breughel of hell.

Translated by Malcolm Cowley

W. H. AUDEN

Refugee Blues

Say this city has ten million souls,
Some are living in mansions, some are living in holes:
Yet there's no place for us, my dear, yet there's no place for
us.

Once we had a country and we thought it fair,
Look in the atlas and you'll find it there:
We cannot go there now, my dear, we cannot go there now.

In the village churchyard there grows an old yew,
Every spring it blossoms anew:
Old passports can't do that, my dear, old passports can't do
that.

The consul banged the table and said,
'If you've got no passport you're officially dead';
But we are still alive, my dear, but we are still alive.

Went to a committee; they offered me a chair;
Asked me politely to return next year:
But where shall we go to-day, my dear, but where shall we
go to-day?

Came to a public meeting: the speaker got up and said;
'If we let them in, they will steal our daily bread':
He was talking of you and me, my dear, he was talking of
you and me.

Thought I heard the thunder rumbling in the sky;
It was Hitler over Europe, saying, 'They must die':
O we were in his mind, my dear. O we were in his mind.

Saw a poodle in a jacket fastened with a pin.
Saw a door opened and a cat let in:
But they weren't German Jews, my dear, but they weren't
    German Jews.

Went down the harbour and stood upon the quay,
Saw the fish swimming as if they were free:
Only ten feet away, my dear, only ten feet away.

Walked through a wood, saw the birds in the trees;
They had no politicians and sang at their ease:
They weren't the human race, my dear, they weren't the
    human race.

Dreamed I saw a building with a thousand floors,
A thousand windows and a thousand doors:
Not one of them was ours, my dear, not one of them was
    ours.

Stood on a great plain in the falling snow;
Ten thousand soldiers marched to and fro:
Looking for you and me, my dear, looking for you and me.

March 1939

September 1, 1939

I sit in one of the dives
On Fifty-Second Street
Uncertain and afraid
As the clever hopes expire
Of a low dishonest decade:
Waves of anger and fear
Circulate over the bright

And darkened lands of the earth,
Obsessing our private lives;
The unmentionable odour of death
Offends the September night.

Accurate scholarship can
Unearth the whole offence
From Luther until now
That has driven a culture mad,
Find what occurred at Linz,
What huge imago made
A psychopathic god:
I and the public know
What all schoolchildren learn,
Those to whom evil is done
Do evil in return.

Exiled Thucydides knew
All that a speech can say
About Democracy,
And what dictators do,
The elderly rubbish they talk
To an apathetic grave;
Analysed all in his book,
The enlightenment driven away,
The habit-forming pain,
Mismanagement and grief:
We must suffer them all again.

Into this neutral air
Where blind skyscrapers use
Their full height to proclaim
The strength of Collective Man,
Each language pours its vain

Competitive excuse:
But who can live for long
In an euphoric dream;
Out of the mirror they stare,
Imperialism's face
And the international wrong.

Faces along the bar
Cling to their average day:
The lights must never go out,
The music must always play,
All the conventions conspire
To make this fort assume
The furniture of home;
Lest we should see where we are,
Lost in a haunted wood,
Children afraid of the night
Who have never been happy or good.

The windiest militant trash
Important Persons shout
Is not so crude as our wish:
What mad Nijinsky wrote
About Diaghilev
Is true of the normal heart;
For the error bred in the bone
Of each woman and each man
Craves what it cannot have,
Not universal love
But to be loved alone.

From the conservative dark
Into the ethical life
The dense commuters come,

Repeating their morning vow,
'I *will* be true to the wife,
I'll concentrate more on my work,'
And helpless governors wake
To resume their compulsory game:
Who can release them now,
Who can reach the deaf,
Who can speak for the dumb?

All I have is a voice
To undo the folded lie,
The romantic lie in the brain
Of the sensual man-in-the-street
And the lie of Authority
Whose buildings grope the sky:
There is no such thing as the State
And no one exists alone;
Hunger allows no choice
To the citizen or the police;
We must love one another or die.

Defenceless under the night
Our world in stupor lies;
Yet, dotted everywhere,
Ironic points of light
Flash out wherever the Just
Exchange their messages:
May I, composed like them
Of Eros and of dust,
Beleaguered by the same
Negation and despair,
Show an affirming flame.

September 1939

[20]

from New Year's Letter

The situation of our time
Surrounds us like a baffling crime:
There lies the body half-undressed,
We all had reason to detest,
And all are suspects and involved
Until the mystery is solved
And under lock and key the cause
That makes a nonsense of our laws.
O Who is trying to shield Whom?
Who left a hairpin in the room?
Who was the distant figure seen
Behaving oddly on the green?
Why did the watchdog never bark?
Why did the footsteps leave no mark?
Where were the servants at that hour?
How did a snake get in the tower?
Delayed in the democracies
By departmental vanities,
The rival sergeants run about
But more to squabble than find out,
Yet where the Force has been cut down
To one inspector dressed in brown,
He makes the murderer whom he pleases
And all investigation ceases.
Yet our equipment all the time
Extends the area of the crime
Until the guilt is everywhere;
And more and more we are aware,
However miserable may be
Our parish of immediacy,

How small it is, how, far beyond,
Ubiquitous within the bond
Of an impoverishing sky,
Vast spiritual disorders lie.
Who, thinking of the last ten years,
Does not hear howling in his ears
The Asiatic cry of pain,
The shots of executing Spain,
See stumbling through his outraged mind
The Abyssinian, blistered, blind,
The dazed uncomprehending stare
Of the Danubian despair,
The Jew wrecked in the German cell,
Flat Poland frozen into hell,
The silent dumps of unemployed
Whose areté has been destroyed;
And will not feel blind anger draw
His thoughts towards the Minotaur,
To take an early boat for Crete
And, rolling, silly, at its feet,
Add his small tid-bit to the rest?
It lures us all; even the best,
Les hommes de bonne volonté, feel
Their politics perhaps unreal
And all they have believed untrue,
Are tempted to surrender to
The grand apocalyptic dream
In which the persecutors scream
As on the evil Aryan lives
Descends the night of the long knives,
The bleeding tyrant dragged through all
The ashes of his capitol.
Though language may be useless, for

No words men write can stop the war
Or measure up to the relief
Of its immeasurable grief,
Yet truth, like love and sleep, resents
Approaches that are too intense,
And often when the searcher stood
Before the Oracle it would
Ignore his grown-up earnestness
But not the child of his distress,
For through the Janus of a joke
The candid psychopompos spoke.

May such heart and intelligence
As huddle now in conference,
Whenever an impasse occurs,
Use the Good Offices of verse;
May an Accord be reached, and may
This aide-mémoire on what they say,
This private minute for a friend,
Be the dispatch that I intend;
Although addressed to a Whitehall,
Be under Flying Seal to all
Who wish to read it anywhere,
And, if they open it, En Clair.

The Shield of Achilles

> She looked over his shoulder
>   For vines and olive trees,
> Marble well-governed cities,
>   And ships upon untamed seas,
> But there on the shining metal
>   His hands had put instead

An artificial wilderness
And a sky like lead.

A plain without a feature, bare and brown
No blade of grass, no sign of neighborhood,
Nothing to eat and nowhere to sit down,
Yet, congregated on its blankness, stood
An unintelligible multitude,
A million eyes, a million boots in line,
Without expression, waiting for a sign.

Out of the air a voice without a face
Proved by statistics that some cause was just
In tones as dry and level as the place:
No one was cheered and nothing was discussed;
Column by column in a cloud of dust
They marched away enduring a belief
Whose logic brought them, somewhere else, to grief.

She looked over his shoulder
For ritual pieties,
White flower-garlanded heifers,
Libation and sacrifice,
But there on the shining metal
Where the altar should have been,
She saw by his flickering forge-light
Quite another scene.

Barbed wire enclosed an arbitrary spot
Where bored officials lounged (one cracked a joke)
And sentries sweated, for the day was hot:
A crowd of ordinary decent folk
Watched from without and neither moved nor spoke
As three pale figures were led forth and bound
To three posts driven upright in the ground.

The mass and majesty of this world, all
  That carries weight and always weighs the same,
Lay in the hands of others; they were small
  And could not hope for help and no help came:
  What their foes liked to do was done, their shame
Was all the worst could wish; they lost their pride
And died as men before their bodies died.

        She looked over his shoulder
            For athletes at their games,
        Men and women in a dance
            Moving their sweet limbs
            Quick, quick, to music,
            But there on the shining shield
        His hands had set no dancing-floor
            But a weed-choked field.

A ragged urchin, aimless and alone,
  Loitered about that vacancy; a bird
Flew up to safety from his well-aimed stone:
  That girls are raped, that two boys knife a third,
  Were axioms to him, who'd never heard
Of any world where promises were kept
Or one could weep because another wept.

        The thin-lipped armorer,
            Hephaestos, hobbled away;
        Thetis of the shining breasts
            Cried out in dismay
        At what the god had wrought
            To please her son, the strong
        Iron-hearted man-slaying Achilles
            Who would not live long.

1952

DONALD BAIN

War Poet

We in our haste can only see the small components of the
  scene
We cannot tell what incidents will focus on the final screen.
A barrage of disruptive sound, a petal on a sleeping face,
Both must be noted, both must have their place;

It may be that our later selves or else our unborn sons
Will search for meaning in the dust of long deserted guns,
We only watch, and indicate and make our scribbled pencil
  notes.
We do not wish to moralise, only to ease our dusty throats.

SAMUEL BECKETT

Saint-Lô

Vire will wind in other shadows
unborn through the bright ways tremble
and the old mind ghost-forsaken
sink into its havoc

1946

Roosters

At four o'clock
in the gun-metal blue dark
we hear the first crow of the first cock

just below
the gun-metal blue window
and immediately there is an echo

off in the distance,
then one from the backyard fence,
then one, with horrible insistence,

grates like a wet match
from the broccoli patch,
flares, and all over town begins to catch.

Cries galore
come from the water-closet door,
from the dropping-plastered henhouse floor,

where in the blue blur
their rustling wives admire,
the roosters brace their cruel feet and glare

with stupid eyes
while from their beaks there rise
the uncontrolled, traditional cries.

Deep from protruding chests
in green-gold medals dressed,
planned to command and terrorise the rest,

the many wives
who lead hens' lives
of being courted and despised;

deep from raw throats
a senseless order floats
all over town. A rooster gloats

over our beds
from rusty iron sheds
and fences made from old bedsteads,

over our churches
where the tin rooster perches,
over our little wooden northern houses,

making sallies
from all the muddy alleys,
marking out maps like Rand McNally's:

glass-headed pins,
oil-golds and copper greens,
anthracite blues, alizarins,

each one an active
displacement in perspective;
each screaming, 'This is where I live!'

Each screaming
'Get up! Stop dreaming!'
Roosters, what are you projecting?

You, whom the Greeks elected
to shoot at on a post, who struggled
when sacrificed, you whom they labeled

'Very combative . . .'
what right have you to give
commands and tell us how to live,

cry 'Here!' and 'Here!'
and wake us here where are
unwanted love, conceit and war?

The crown of red
set on your little head
is charged with all your fighting blood.

Yes, that excrescence
makes a most virile presence,
plus all that vulgar beauty of iridescence.

Now in mid-air
by twos they fight each other.
Down comes a first flame-feather,

and one is flying,
with raging heroism defying
even the sensation of dying.

And one has fallen,
but still above the town
his torn-out, bloodied feathers drift down;

and what he sung
no matter. He is flung
on the gray ash-heap, lies in dung

with his dead wives
with open, bloody eyes,
while those metallic feathers oxidise.

St Peter's sin
was worse than that of Magdalen
whose sin was of the flesh alone;

of spirit, Peter's,
falling, beneath the flares,
among the 'servants and officers.'

Old holy sculpture
could set it all together
in one small scene, past and future:

Christ stands amazed,
Peter, two fingers raised
to surprised lips, both as if dazed.

But in between
a little cock is seen
carved on a dim column in the travertine,

explained by *gallus canit;*
flet Petrus underneath it.
There is inescapable hope, the pivot;

yes, and there Peter's tears
run down our chanticleer's
sides and gem his spurs.

Tear-encrusted thick
as a medieval relic
he waits. Poor Peter, heart-sick,

still cannot guess
those cock-a-doodles yet might bless,
his dreadful rooster come to mean forgiveness,

a new weathervane
on basilica and barn,
and that outside the Lateran

there would always be
a bronze cock on a porphyry
pillar so the people and the Pope might see

that even the Prince
of the Apostles long since
had been forgiven, and to convince

all the assembly
that 'Deny deny deny'
is not all the roosters cry.

In the morning
a low light is floating
in the backyard, and gilding

from underneath
the broccoli, leaf by leaf;
how could the night have come to grief?

gilding the tiny
floating swallow's belly
and lines of pink cloud in the sky,

the day's preamble
like wandering lines in marble.
The cocks are now almost inaudible.

The sun climbs in,
following 'to see the end,'
faithful as enemy, or friend.

JOHANNES BOBROWSKI

North Russian Town
(Pustoshka 1941)

Pale
by the road to the North
falls the mountain-wall. The bridge,
the old wood,
the bushy banks.

There the stream lives,
white in the pebbles, blind over the
sand. And the caw of crows
speaks your name: Wind
in the rafters, a smoke
towards the evening.

It comes,
glowing in
the cloud, it follows the winds,
it watches for the fire.

Remote fire breaks forth
in the plain,
far. Who dwell near
forests, on streams, in the wooden
luck of the villages, listen
at evening, lay
an ear to the earth.

Translated from the German by Matthew and Ruth Mead

Report

Bajla Gelblung,
escaped in Warsaw
from a transport from the Ghetto,
the girl took to the woods,
armed, was picked up
as partisan
in Brest-Litovsk,
wore a military coat (Polish),
was interrogated by German
officers, there is
a photo, the officers are young
chaps faultlessly uniformed,
with faultless faces,
their bearing
is unexceptionable.

Translated by Matthew and Ruth Mead

BERTOLT BRECHT

Bad Time for Poetry

Yes, I know: only the happy man
Is liked. His voice
Is good to hear. His face is handsome.

The crippled tree in the yard
Shows that the soil is poor, yet
The passers-by abuse it for being crippled
And rightly so.

The green boats and the dancing sails on the Sound
Go unseen. Of it all
I see only the torn nets of the fishermen.
Why do I only record
That a village woman aged forty walks with a stoop?
The girls' breasts
Are as warm as ever.

In my poetry a rhyme
Would seem to me almost insolent.

Inside me contend
Delight at the apple tree in blossom
And horror at the house-painter's speeches.
But only the second
Drives me to my desk.

*Translated from the German by John Willett
and Ralph Manheim*

This Summer's Sky

High above the lake a bomber flies.
From the rowing boats
Children look up, women, an old man. From a distance
They appear like young starlings, their beaks
Wide open for food.

Translated by Michael Hamburger

The Friends

The war separated
Me, the writer of plays, from my friend the stage designer.
The cities where we worked are no longer there.
When I walk through the cities that still are
At times I say: that blue piece of washing
My friend would have placed it better.

Translated by Michael Hamburger

1940

I

Spring is coming. The gentle winds
Are freeing the cliffs of their winter ice.
Trembling, the peoples of the north await
The battle fleets of the house-painter.

II

Out of the libraries
Emerge the butchers.
Pressing their children closer
Mothers stand and humbly search
The skies for the inventions of learned men.

III

The designers sit
Hunched in the drawing offices:
One wrong figure, and the enemy's cities
Will remain undestroyed.

IV

Fog envelops
The road
The poplars
The farms and
The artillery.

V

I am now living on the small island of Lidingö.
But one night recently
I had heavy dreams and I dreamed I was in a city
And discovered that its street signs
Were in German. I awoke
Bathed in sweat, saw the fir tree
Black as night before my window, and realised with relief:
I was in a foreign land.

VI

My young son asks me: Should I learn mathematics?
What for, I'm inclined to say. That two bits of bread are
   more than one
You'll notice anyway.
My young son asks me: Should I learn French?
What for, I'm inclined to say. That empire is going under.
Just rub your hand across your belly and groan
And you'll be understood all right.
My young son asks me: Should I learn history?
What for, I'm inclined to say. Learn to stick your head in the
   ground
Then maybe you'll come through.

Yes, learn mathematics, I tell him
Learn French, learn history!

In front of the whitewashed wall
Stands the black military case with the manuscripts.
On it lie the smoking things with the copper ashtrays.
The Chinese scroll depicting the Doubter
Hangs above it. The masks are there too. And by the
   bedstead
Stands the little six-valve radio.
Mornings

I turn it on and hear
The victory bulletins of my enemies.

Fleeing from my fellow-countrymen
I have now reached Finland. Friends
Whom yesterday I didn't know, put up some beds
In clean rooms. Over the radio
I hear the victory bulletins of the scum of the earth.
   Curiously
I examine a map of the continent. High up in Lapland
Towards the Arctic Ocean
I can still see a small door.

Translated by Sammy McLean

Song of a German Mother

My son, your shiny boots and
Brown shirt were a present from me:
If I'd known then what I know now
I'd have hanged myself from a tree.
My son, when I saw your hand raised
In the Hitler salute that first day
I didn't know those who saluted
Would see their hand wither away.

My son, I can hear your voice speaking:
Of a race of heroes it tells.
I didn't know, guess or see that
You worked in their torture cells.

My son, when I saw you marching
In Hitler's victorious train
I didn't know he who marched off then
Would never come back again.

My son, you told me our country
Was about to come into its own.
I didn't know all it would come to
Was ashes and bloodstained stone.

I saw you wearing your brown shirt.
I should have protested aloud
For I did not know what I now know:
It was your burial shroud.

Translated by John Willett

War Has Been Given a Bad Name

I am told that the best people have begun saying
How, from a moral point of view, the Second World War
Fell below the standard of the First. The Wehrmacht
Allegedly deplores the methods by which the SS effected
The extermination of certain peoples. The Ruhr industrialists
Are said to regret the bloody manhunts
Which filled their mines and factories with slave workers.
    The intellectuals
So I heard, condemn industry's demand for slave workers
Likewise their unfair treatment. Even the bishops
Dissociate themselves from this way of waging war; in short
    the feeling
Prevails in every quarter that the Nazis did the Fatherland
A lamentably bad turn, and that war
While in itself natural and necessary, has, thanks to the
Unduly uninhibited and positively inhuman
Way in which it was conducted on this occasion, been
Discredited for some time to come.

Translated by John Willett

Epistle to the Augsburgers

And then when it was the month of May
A Thousand-year Reich had passed away.

And down the street called Hindenburggass'
Came boys from Missouri with bazookas and cameras

Seeking the way, and what loot they could take
And one single German who thought World War II a
mistake.

The Mis-Leader lay under the Chancellery
Of low-browed corpses with little moustaches there were
two or three.

Field Marshals were rotting along the pavement
Butcher asked butcher to pass judgement.

The vetches flowered. The cocks were quietly moping.
The doors were closed. The roofs stood open.

Translated by Lesley Lendrum

NORMAN CAMERON

Green, Green is El Aghir

Sprawled on the crates and sacks in the rear of the truck,
I was gummy-mouthed from the sun and the dust of the
    track.
And the two Arab soldiers I'd taken on as hitch-hikers
At a torrid petrol-dump, had been there on their hunkers
Since early morning. I said, in a kind of French
'On m'a dit, qu'il y a une belle source d'eau fraîche.
Plus loin, à El Aghir' . . .

      It was eighty more kilometres
Until round a corner we heard a splashing of waters,
And there, in a green, dark street, was a fountain with two
    faces
Discharging both ways, from full-throated faucets
Into basins, thence into troughs and thence into brooks.
Our negro corporal driver slammed his brakes,
And we yelped and leapt from the truck and went at the
    double
To fill our bidons and bottles and drink and dabble.
Then, swollen with water, we went to an inn for wine.
The Arabs came, too, though their faith might have stood
    between.
'After all,' they said, 'it's a boisson,' without contrition.

Green, green is El Aghir. It has a railway-station,
And the wealth of its soil has borne many another fruit,
A mairie, a school and an elegant Salle de Fêtes.
Such blessings, as I remarked, in effect, to the waiter,
Are added unto them that have plenty of water.

DAVID CAMPBELL

Men in Green

There were fifteen men in green,
Each with a tommy-gun,
Who leapt into my plane at dawn;
We rose to meet the sun.

Our course lay to the east. We climbed
Into the break of day,
Until the jungle far beneath
Like a giant fossil lay.

We climbed towards the distant range
Where two white paws of cloud
Clutched at the shoulders of the pass.
The green men laughed aloud.

They did not fear the ape-like cloud
That climbed the mountain crest
And rode the currents of the air
And hid the pass in mist.

They did not fear the summer's sun
In whose hot centre lie
A hundred hissing cannon shells
For the unwatchful eye.

And when at Dobadura we
Set down, each turned to raise
His thumb towards the open sky
In mockery and praise.

But fifteen men in jungle green
Rose from the kunai grass
To come aboard, and my green men
In silence watched them pass:
It seemed they looked upon themselves
In a prophetic glass.

There were some leaned on a stick
And some on stretchers lay,
But few walked on their own two feet
In the early green of day.

They had not feared the ape-like cloud
That climbed the mountain crest;
They had not feared the summer's sun
With bullets for their breast.

JEAN CASSOU

from Sonnets of the Resistance: 13

Cutting a sky of chalk the steep road goes
to the blue laundry. Only you are there,
pilgrim of pallid cobbles, from some square
where benches creak and kiosks decompose.

Numb shock hangs painted where your eyes enquire:
the frozen cry of placards, the congealed
windows of clapped-out shops, the target-field
of housefronts waiting for the burst of fire!

Get off the road, get out of every road:
you never found that future you were owed!
Deep silence is the echo of your tread.

Let roofs and windows laugh in ecstasies,
let parks of kings shake off your presence dead,
beneath whose ashen weight they cannot rise!

Translated from the French by Timothy Adès

CHARLES CAUSLEY

Conversation in Gibraltar 1943

We sit here, talking of Barea and Lorca
Meeting the iron eye of the Spanish clock.
We have cut, with steel bows, the jungle of salt-water,
Sustaining the variable sea-fevers of home and women,
To walk the blazing ravine
Of the profitable Rock.

We hold, in our pockets, no comfortable return tickets:
Only the future, gaping like some hideous fable.
The antique Mediterranean of history and Alexander,
The rattling galley and the young Greek captains
Are swept up and piled
Under the table.

We have walked to Europa and looked east to the invisible
    island,
The bitter rock biting the heel through the shoe-leather.
Rain's vague infantry, the Levant, parachutes on the stone
    lion
And soon, soon, under our feet and the thin steel deck
We shall be conscious of miles of perpendicular sea,
And the Admiralty weather.

PAUL CELAN

Nearness of Graves

Still do the southerly Bug waters know,
Mother, the wave whose blows wounded you so?

Still does the field with those windmills remember
how gently your heart to its angels surrendered?

Can none of the aspens and none of the willows
allow you their solace, remove all your sorrows?

And does not the god with his blossoming wand
go up in the hills climbing hither and yon?

And can you bear, Mother, as once on a time,
the gentle, the German, the pain-laden rhyme?

Translated from the German by John Felstiner

'Aspen tree'

Aspen tree, your leaves glance white into the dark.
My mother's hair never turned white.

Dandelion, so green is the Ukraine.
My fair-haired mother did not come home.

Rain cloud, do you linger at the well?
My soft-voiced mother weeps for all.

Rounded star, you coil the golden loop.
My mother's heart was hurt by lead.

Oaken door, who hove you off your hinge?
My gentle mother cannot return.

Translated by John Felstiner

Deathfugue

Black milk of daybreak we drink it at evening
we drink it at midday and morning we drink it at night
we drink and we drink
we shovel a grave in the air where you won't lie too cramped
A man lives in the house he plays with his vipers he writes
he writes when it grows dark to Deutschland your golden
    hair Margareta
he writes it and steps out of doors and the stars are all
    sparkling he whistles his hounds to stay close
he whistles his Jews into rows has them shovel a grave in the
    ground
he commands us play up for the dance

Black milk of daybreak we drink you at night
we drink you at morning and midday we drink you at
    evening
we drink and we drink
A man lives in the house he plays with his vipers he writes
he writes when it grows dark to Deutschland your golden
    hair Margareta
Your ashen hair Shulamith we shovel a grave in the air
    where you won't lie too cramped

He shouts dig this earth deeper you lot there you others sing
    up and play
he grabs for the rod in his belt he swings it his eyes are so
    blue

[48]

stick your spades deeper you lot there you others play on for
the dancing

Black milk of daybreak we drink you at night
we drink you at midday and morning we drink you at
evening
we drink and we drink
a man lives in the house your goldenes Haar Margareta
your aschenes Haar Shulamith he plays with his vipers

He shouts play death more sweetly this Death is a master
from Deutschland
he shouts scrape your strings darker you'll rise up as smoke
to the sky
you'll then have a grave in the clouds where you won't lie
too cramped

Black milk of daybreak we drink you at night
we drink you at midday Death is a master aus Deutschland
we drink you at evening and morning we drink and we drink
this Death is ein Meister aus Deutschland his eye it is blue
he shoots you with shot made of lead shoots you level and
true
a man lives in the house your goldenes Haar Margarete
he looses his hounds on us grants us a grave in the air
he plays with his vipers and daydreams der Tod ist ein
Meister aus Deutschland

dein goldenes Haar Margarete
dein aschenes Haar Sulamith

Translated by John Felstiner

ALICE COATS

The 'Monstrous Regiment'

What hosts of women everywhere I see!
I'm sick to death of them – and they of me.
(The few remaining men are small and pale–
War lends a spurious value to the male.)
Mechanics are supplanted by their mothers;
Aunts take the place of artisans and others;
Wives sell the sago, daughters drive the van,
Even the mansion is without a man!
Females are farming who were frail before,
Matrons attending meetings by the score,
Maidens are minding multiple machines,
And virgins vending station-magazines.
Dames, hoydens, wenches, harridans and hussies
Cram to congestion all the trams and buses;
Misses and grandmas, mistresses and nieces,
Infest bombed buildings, picking up the pieces.

Girls from the South and lassies from the North,
Sisters and sweethearts, bustle back and forth.
The newsboy and the boy who drives the plough:
Postman and milkman – all are ladies now.
Doctors and engineers – yes, even these–
Poets and politicians, all are shes.
(The very beasts that in the meadows browse
Are ewes and mares, heifers and hens and cows . . .)
All, doubtless, worthy to a high degree;
But oh, how boring! Yes, including me.

Disintegration of Springtime

This is a damned unnatural sort of war;
The pilot sits among the clouds, quite sure
About the values he is fighting for;
He cannot hear beyond his veil of sound,

He cannot see the people on the ground;
He only knows that on the sloping map
Of sea-fringed town and country people creep
Like ants – and who cares if ants laugh or weep?

To us he is no more than a machine
Shown on an instrument; what can he mean
In human terms? – a man, somebody's son,
Proud of his skill; compact of flesh and bone
Fragile as Icarus – and our desire
To see that damned machine come down on fire.

Unseen Fire

This is a damned inhuman sort of war.
I have been fighting in a dressing-gown
Most of the night; I cannot see the guns,
The sweating gun-detachments or the planes;

I sweat down here before a symbol thrown
Upon a screen, sift facts, initiate
Swift calculations and swift orders; wait
For the precise split-second to order fire.

We chant our ritual words; beyond the phones
A ghost repeats the orders to the guns:
One Fire . . . Two Fire . . . ghosts answer: the guns roar
Abruptly; and an aircraft waging war
Inhumanly from nearly five miles height
Meets our bouquet of death – and turns sharp right.

ROBERT DESNOS

Epitaph

I lived in those times. For a thousand years
I have been dead. Not fallen, but hunted;
When all human decency was imprisoned,
I was free amongst the masked slaves.

I lived in those times, yet I was free.
I watched the river, the earth, the sky,
Turning around me, keeping their balance.
The seasons provided their birds and their honey.

You who live, what have you made of your luck?
Do you regret the time when I struggled?
Have you cultivated for the common harvest?
Have you enriched the town I lived in?

Living men, think nothing of me. I am dead.
Nothing survives of my spirit or my body.

Translated from the French by Kenneth Rexroth

The Plague

A footstep echoes in the street. The bell has only one
clapper. Where is he going the walker who's coming slowly
closer and abruptly stops. He's just in front
of the house. I can hear his breath behind the door.

I can see the sky through the glass. I can see the sky where
    the
stars wheel round over the roofs' ridge. There's the Great

[53]

Bear or Betelgeuse, there's Venus with her white belly, there's
Diana unhooking her tunic by a fountain of light.

The moons and suns have never wheeled so far from the
earth. The night air has never been so opaque
or so heavy. I lean on the resistant door . . .

In the end it opens and its panels clack against
the wall. As the footsteps fade, I decipher
black letters on a yellow poster spelling 'PLAGUE'.

Translated by Hugh Haughton

KEITH DOUGLAS

Simplify me when I'm dead

Remember me when I am dead
and simplify me when I'm dead.

As the processes of earth
strip off the colour and the skin
take the brown hair and blue eye

and leave me simpler than at birth,
when hairless I came howling in
as the moon came in the cold sky.

Of my skeleton perhaps
so stripped, a learned man will say
'He was of such a type and intelligence,' no more.

Thus when in a year collapse
particular memories, you may
deduce, from the long pain I bore

the opinions I held, who was my foe
and what I left, even my appearance
but incidents will be no guide.

Time's wrong-way telescope will show
a minute man ten years hence
and by distance simplified.

Through that lens see if I seem
substance or nothing: of the world
deserving mention or charitable oblivion

not by momentary spleen
or love into decision hurled,
leisurely arrive at an opinion.

Remember me when I am dead
and simplify me when I'm dead.

Dead Men

Tonight the moon inveigles them
to love: they infer from her gaze
her tacit encouragement.
Tonight the white dresses and the jasmin scent
in the streets. I in another place
see the white dresses glimmer like moths. Come

to the west, out of that trance, my heart—
here the same hours have illumined
sleepers who are condemned or reprieved
and those whom their ambitions have deceived;
the dead men, whom the wind
powders till they are like dolls: they tonight

rest in the sanitary earth perhaps
or where they died, no one has found them
or in their shallow graves the wild dog
discovered and exhumed a face or a leg
for food: the human virtue round them
is a vapour tasteless to a dog's chops.

All that is good of them, the dog consumes.
You would not know, now the mind's flame is gone,
more than the dog knows: you would forget
but that you see your own mind burning yet

and till you stifle in the ground will go on
burning the economical coal of your dreams.

Then leave the dead in the earth, an organism
not capable of resurrection, like mines,
less durable than the metal of a gun,
a casual meal for a dog, nothing but the bone
so soon. But tonight no lovers see the lines
of the moon's face as the lines of cynicism.

And the wise man is the lover
who in his planetary love revolves
without the traction of reason or time's control
and the wild dog finding meat in a hole
is a philosopher. The prudent mind resolves
on the lover's or the dog's attitude for ever.

Cairo Jag

Shall I get drunk or cut myself a piece of cake,
a pasty Syrian with a few words of English
or the Turk who says she is a princess – she dances
apparently by levitation? Or Marcelle, Parisienne
always preoccupied with her dull dead lover:
she has all the photographs and his letters
tied in a bundle and stamped *Décedé* in mauve ink.
All this takes place in a stink of jasmin.

But there are the streets dedicated to sleep
stenches and the sour smells, the sour cries
do not disturb their application to slumber
all day, scattered on the pavement like rags
afflicted with fatalism and hashish. The women

offering their children brown-paper breasts
dry and twisted, elongated like the skull,
Holbein's signature. But this stained white town
is something in accordance with mundane conventions–
Marcelle drops her Gallic airs and tragedy
suddenly shrieks in Arabic about the fare
with the cabman, links herself so
with the somnambulists and legless beggars:
it is all one, all as you have heard.

But by a day's travelling you reach a new world
the vegetation is of iron
dead tanks, gun barrels split like celery
the metal brambles have no flowers or berries
and there are all sorts of manure, you can imagine
the dead themselves, their boots, clothes and possessions
clinging to the ground, a man with no head
has a packet of chocolate and a souvenir of Tripoli.

Desert Flowers

Living in a wide landscape are the flowers–
Rosenberg I only repeat what you were saying–
the shell and the hawk every hour
are slaying men and jerboas, slaying

the mind: but the body can fill
the hungry flowers and the dogs who cry words
at nights, the most hostile things of all.
But that is not new. Each time the night discards

draperies on the eyes and leaves the mind awake
I look each side of the door of sleep

for the little coin it will take
to buy the secret I shall not keep.

I see men as trees suffering
or confound the detail and the horizon.
Lay the coin on my tongue and I will sing
of what the others never set eyes on.

Landscape with Figures

1

Perched on a great fall of air
a pilot or angel looking down
on some eccentric chart, the plain
dotted with the useless furniture
discerns crouching on the sand vehicles
squashed dead or still entire, stunned
like beetles: scattered wingcases and
legs, heads, show when the haze settles.
But you who like Thomas come
to poke fingers in the wounds
find monuments, and metal posies:
on each disordered tomb
the steel is torn into fronds
by the lunatic explosive.

2

On scrub and sand the dead men wriggle
in their dowdy clothes. They are mimes
who express silence and futile aims
enacting this prone and motionless struggle

at a queer angle to the scenery
crawling on the boards of the stage like walls
deaf to the one who opens his mouth and calls
silently. The décor is terrible tracery
of iron. The eye and mouth of each figure
bear the cosmetic blood and hectic
colours death has the only list of.
A yard more, and my little finger
could trace the maquillage of these stony actors
I am the figure writhing on the backcloth.

Vergissmeinnicht

Three weeks gone and the combatants gone
returning over the nightmare ground
we found the place again, and found
the soldier sprawling in the sun.

The frowning barrel of his gun
overshadowing. As we came on
that day, he hit my tank with one
like the entry of a demon.

Look. Here in the gunpit spoil
the dishonoured picture of his girl
who has put: *Steffi. Vergissmeinnicht*
in a copybook gothic script.

We see him almost with content,
abased, and seeming to have paid
and mocked at by his own equipment
that's hard and good when he's decayed.

But she would weep to see today
how on his skin the swart flies move;

the dust upon the paper eye
and the burst stomach like a cave.

For here the lover and killer are mingled
who had one body and one heart.
And death who had the soldier singled
has done the lover mortal hurt.

Tunisia, 1943

Jerusalem

Tonight there is a movement of things
the cat moonlight leaps out
between the dark hotels upon
the river of people; is gone
and in the dark words fall about.
In the dome of stars the moon sings.

Ophelia, in a pool of shadow lies
your face, flower that draws down my lips
our hands meet like strangers in a city
among the glasses on the table-top
impervious to envy or pity
we two lost in the country of our eyes.

We two, and other twos.
Stalingrad, Pacific, Tunis,
Tripoli, the many heads of war
are watching us. But now, and here
is night's short forgiveness
that all lovers use.

Now the dark theatre of the sky
encloses the conversation of the whole city

islanded, we sit under
the vault of it, and wonder
to hear such music in the petty
laughter and talk of passers-by.

How to Kill

Under the parabola of a ball,
a child turning into a man,
I looked into the air too long.
The ball fell in my hand, it sang
in the closed fist: *Open Open*
Behold a gift designed to kill.

Now in my dial of glass appears
the soldier who is going to die.
He smiles, and moves about in ways
his mother knows, habits of his.
The wires touch his face: I cry
NOW. Death, like a familiar, hears

and look, has made a man of dust
of a man of flesh. This sorcery
I do. Being damned, I am amused
to see the centre of love diffused
and the waves of love travel into vacancy.
How easy it is to make a ghost.

The weightless mosquito touches
her tiny shadow on the stone,
and with how like, how infinite
a lightness, man and shadow meet.
They fuse. A shadow is a man
when the mosquito death approaches.

RICHARD EBERHART

The Fury of Aerial Bombardment

You would think the fury of aerial bombardment
Would rouse God to relent; the infinite spaces
Are still silent. He looks on shock-pried faces.
History, even, does not know what is meant.

You would feel that after so many centuries
God would give man to repent; yet he can kill
As Cain could, but with multitudinous will,
No farther advanced than in his ancient furies.

Was man made stupid to see his own stupidity?
Is God by definition indifference, beyond us all?
Is the eternal truth man's fighting soul
Wherein the Beast ravens in its own avidity?

Of Van Wettering I speak, and Averill,
Names on a list, whose faces I do not recall
But they are gone to early death, who late in school
Distinguished the belt feed lever from the belt holding pawl.

GÜNTER EICH

Inventory

This is my cap,
this is my greatcoat,
and here's my shaving kit
in its linen bag.

A can of meat:
my plate, my mug,
into its tin
I've scratched my name.

Scratched it with this
invaluable nail
which I keep hidden
from covetous eyes.

My bread bag holds
two woollen socks
and a couple of things
I show to no one.

like that it serves me
as a pillow at night.
Between me and the earth
I lay this cardboard.

This pencil lead
is what I love most:
by day it writes verses
I thought up in the night.

This is my notebook
and this is my groundsheet,
this is my towel,
this is my thread.

1948, Abgelegene Gehöfte

Translated from the German by Michael Hamburger

Geometrical Place

We have sold our shadow,
it hangs on a wall in Hiroshima,
a transaction we knew nothing of,
from which, embarrassed, we rake in interest.

And, dear friends, drink my whiskey,
I won't be able to find the tavern any more,
where my bottle stands
with its monogram,
old proof of a clear conscience.

I didn't put my penny in the bank
when Christ was born
but I've seen the grandchildren
of dogs trained to herd people
on the hills near the Danube School,
and they stared at me.

And I want, like the people of Hiroshima,
to see no more burnt skin,
I want to drink and sing songs,
to sing for whiskey,
and to stroke the dogs, whose grandfathers

sprang at people
in quarries and barbed wire.

You, my shadow,
on the bank at Hiroshima,
I want to visit you with all the dogs
now and then
and drink to you
to the prosperity of our accounts.

The museum is being demolished,
in front of it
I will slip to you
behind your railing,
behind your smile – our cry for help –
and we'll suit each other again,
your shoes into mine
precise
to the second.

Translated by Stuart Friebert

T. S. ELIOT

Defence of the Islands

Defence of the Islands cannot pretend to be verse, but its date –
just after the evacuation from Dunkirk – and occasion have for
me a significance which makes me wish to preserve it. McKnight
Kauffer was then working for the Ministry of Information. At
his request I wrote these lines to accompany an exhibition in
New York of photographs illustrating the war effort of Britain.
They were subsequently published in Britain At War *(the*
Museum of Modern Art, New York 1941). I now dedicate them
to the memory of Edward McKnight Kauffer.

Let these memorials of built stone – music's
enduring instrument, of many centuries of
patient cultivation of the earth, of English
verse

be joined with the memory of this defence of
the islands

and the memory of those appointed to the grey
ships – battleship, merchantman, trawler–
contributing their share to the ages' pavement
of British bone on the sea floor

and of those who, in man's newest form of gamble
with death, fight the power of darkness in air
and fire

and of those who have followed their forebears
to Flanders and France, those undefeated in de-
feat, unalterable in triumph, changing nothing
of their ancestors' ways but the weapons
and those again for whom the paths of glory are
the lanes and the streets of Britain:

to say, to the past and the future generations
of our kin and of our speech, that we took up
our positions, in obedience to instructions.

A Note on War Poetry

A Note on War Poetry *was written at the request of Miss Storm Jameson, to be included in a book entitled* London Calling *(Harper Brothers, New York, 1942).*

Not the expression of collective emotion
Imperfectly reflected in the daily papers.
Where is the point at which the merely individual
Explosion breaks

In the path of an action merely typical
To create the universal, originate a symbol
Out of the impact? This is a meeting
On which we attend

Of forces beyond control by experiment—
Of Nature and the Spirit. Mostly the individual
Experience is too large, or too small. Our emotions
Are only 'incidents'

In the effort to keep day and night together.
It seems just possible that a poem might happen
To a very young man: but a poem is not poetry—
That is a life.

War is not a life: it is a situation,
One which may neither be ignored nor accepted,
A problem to be met with ambush and stratagem,
Enveloped or scattered.

The enduring is not a substitute for the transient,
Neither one for the other. But the abstract conception

Of private experience at its greatest intensity
Becoming universal, which we call 'poetry',
May be affirmed in verse.

from Little Gidding

II

Ash on an old man's sleeve
Is all the ash the burnt roses leave.
Dust in the air suspended
Marks the place where a story ended.
Dust inbreathed was a house –
The wall, the wainscot and the mouse.
The death of hope and despair,
    This is the death of air.

There are flood and drouth
Over the eyes and in the mouth,
Dead water and dead sand
Contending for the upper hand.
The parched eviscerate soil
Gapes at the vanity of toil,
Laughs without mirth.
    This is the death of earth.

Water and fire succeed
The town, the pasture and the weed.
Water and fire deride
The sacrifice that we denied.
Water and fire shall rot
The marred foundations we forgot,
Of sanctuary and choir.
    This is the death of water and fire.

In the uncertain hour before the morning
   Near the ending of interminable night
   At the recurrent end of the unending
After the dark dove with the flickering tongue
   Had passed below the horizon of his homing
   While the dead leaves still rattled on like tin
Over the asphalt where no other sound was
   Between three districts whence the smoke arose
   I met one walking, loitering and hurried
As if blown towards me like the metal leaves
   Before the urban dawn wind unresisting.
   And as I fixed upon the down-turned face
That pointed scrutiny with which we challenge
   The first-met stranger in the waning dusk
   I caught the sudden look of some dead master
Whom I had known, forgotten, half recalled
   Both one and many; in the brown baked features
   The eyes of a familiar compound ghost
Both intimate and unidentifiable.
   So I assumed a double part, and cried
   And heard another's voice cry: 'What! are *you* here?'
Although we were not. I was still the same,
   Knowing myself yet being someone other –
   And he a face still forming; yet the words sufficed
To compel the recognition they preceded.
   And so, compliant to the common wind,
   Too strange to each other for misunderstanding,
In concord at this intersection time
   Of meeting nowhere, no before and after,
   We trod the pavement in a dead patrol.
I said: 'The wonder that I feel is easy,
   Yet ease is cause of wonder. Therefore speak:
   I may not comprehend, may not remember.'

And he: 'I am not eager to rehearse
  My thoughts and theory which you have forgotten.
  These things have served their purpose: let them be.
So with your own, and pray they be forgiven
  By others, as I pray you to forgive
  Both bad and good. Last season's fruit is eaten
And the fullfed beast shall kick the empty pail.
  For last year's words belong to last year's language
  And next year's words await another voice.
But, as the passage now presents no hindrance
  To the spirit unappeased and peregrine
  Between two worlds become much like each other,
So I find words I never thought to speak
  In streets I never thought I should revisit
  When I left my body on a distant shore.
Since our concern was speech, and speech impelled us
  To purify the dialect of the tribe
  And urge the mind to aftersight and foresight,
Let me disclose the gifts reserved for age
  To set a crown upon your lifetime's effort.
  First, the cold friction of expiring sense
Without enchantment, offering no promise
  But bitter tastelessness of shadow fruit
  As body and soul begin to fall asunder.
Second, the conscious impotence of rage
  At human folly, and the laceration
  Of laughter at what ceases to amuse.
And last, the rending pain of re-enactment
  Of all that you have done, and been; the shame
  Of motives late revealed, and the awareness
Of things ill done and done to others' harm
  Which once you took for exercise of virtue.
  Then fools' approval stings, and honour stains.

From wrong to wrong the exasperated spirit
  Proceeds, unless restored by that refining fire
  Where you must move in measure, like a dancer.'
The day was breaking. In the disfigured street
  He left me, with a kind of valediction,
  And faded on the blowing of the horn.

PAUL ÉLUARD

Courage

Paris is cold Paris is hungry
Paris no longer eats chestnuts in the streets
Paris has put on an old woman's old clothes
Paris sleeps standing airless in the Metro
More misery still is heaped upon the poor
And the wisdom and the folly
Of unhappy Paris
Are the fire and the pure air
Are the beauty and the goodness
Of her hungry toilers
Do not cry for help Paris
You are alive with a life without equal
And behind the bareness
Of your pallor and your thinness
All that is human is revealed in your eyes
Paris my handsome city
Sharp as a needle strong as a sword
Artless and erudite
You do not bear injustice
For you it is the only chaos
You will free yourself Paris
Paris twinkling like a star
Our surviving hope
You will free yourself from dirt and weariness
Brothers let us have courage
We who are not helmeted
Nor booted nor gloved nor well brought up
A ray lights up in our veins

Our light comes back to us
The best of us have died for us
And their blood now finds again our hearts
And it is morning once more a Paris morning
The dawn of deliverance
The space of spring new born
Senseless force has the worst of it
These slaves our enemies
If they have understood
If they are capable of understanding
Will rise up.

1942

Translated from the French by Gilbert Bowen

In April 1944: Paris Was Still Breathing!

We came down to the faithful river: neither its flood nor our
eyes forsook Paris.

Not a mean city, but a city childlike and motherly.

*

A city like a winding path in summer, filled with flowers and
birds, like a long kiss filled with smiling children, filled
with delicate mothers.

Not a city despoiled, but a bewildering city, bearing her
nakedness.

*

A city between our hands like a broken bond, between our
eyes like an eye already seen, a city sung again like a
poem.

[74]

A city built in our own image.

*

An old city . . . Between the city and man there remained not
even the thickness of a wall.

*

A city of transparence, a guiltless city.

*

Between man alone and the deserted city there was nothing
but the thickness of a mirror.

Nothing but a city in the colours of man, earth and flesh,
blood and strength.

*

The day that plays in the water, the night that dies on earth.
The rhythm of pure air is stronger than war.

A city with an outstretched hand, and then comes all the
laughing world and all the revelling world, a city to
behold.

*

No one could hurl down the bridges that led us to sleep and
from sleep to our dreams and from our dreams to eternity.

An enduring city where I have lived through our victory over
death.

1945

Translated by Gilbert Bowen

ODYSSEUS ELYTIS

from Heroic and Elegiac Song for the Lost Second
Lieutenant of the Albanian Campaign (1945)

III

For those men night was a more bitter day
They melted iron, chewed the earth
Their God smelled of gunpowder and mule-hide

Each thunderclap was a death riding the sky
Each thunderclap a man smiling in the face
Of death – let fate say what she will.

Suddenly the moment misfired and struck courage
Hurled splinters head-on into the sun
Binoculars, sights, mortars, froze with terror.

Easily, like calico that the wind rips
Easily, like lungs that stones have punctured
The helmet rolled to the left side . . .

For one moment only roots shook in the soil
Then the smoke dissolved and the day tried timidly
To beguile the infernal tumult.

But night rose up like a spurned viper
Death paused one second on the brink –
Then struck deeply with his pallid claws.

IV

Now with a still wind in his quiet hair
A twig of forgetfulness at his left ear

He lies on the scorched cape
Like a garden the birds have suddenly deserted
Like a song gagged in the darkness
Like an angel's watch that has stopped
Eyelashes barely whispered goodbye
And bewilderment became rigid . . .

He lies on the scorched cape
Black ages round him
Bay at the terrible silence with dog's skeletons
And hours that have once more turned into stone pigeons
Listen attentively.
But laughter is burnt, earth has grown deaf,
No one heard that last, that final cry
The whole world emptied with that very last cry.

Beneath the five cedars
Without other candles
He lies on the scorched cape.
The helmet is empty, the blood full of dirt,
At his side the arm half shot away
And between the eyebrows –
Small bitter spring, fingerprint of fate
Small bitter red-black spring
Spring where memory freezes.

O do not look O do not look at the place where life
Where life has left him. Do not say
Do not say how the smoke of dream has risen
This is the way one moment this is the way
This is the way one moment deserts the other
And this is the way the all-powerful sun suddenly deserts the
    world.

Bring new hands, for now who will ascend
To sing lullabies to the stars' children.
Bring new limbs, for now who will be the first
To join in the dance of the angels.
New eyes – O my God – for now
Who will stoop to the lilies of the beloved.
New blood, for with what joyful greeting will they take fire
And mouth, fresh mouth of bronze and amaranth
For now who will bid the clouds goodbye.

Day, who will confront the peachleaves
Night, who will tame the wheatfields
Who will scatter green candles over the plains
Or cry out courageously in the face of the sun
To clothe himself in storms astride the invulnerable horse
To become the Achilles of the shipyards.
Who will go to the mythical black island
To kiss the pebbles
And who will sleep
To pass through the gulfs of dream
To find new hands, limbs, eyes
Blood and speech
To stand again on the marble threshing floors
And with his holiness grapple – ah, this time –
Grapple with Death.

Translated from the Greek by Edmund Keeley
and Philip Sherrard

Reflection from Rochester
'But wretched Man is still in arms for Fear.'

'From fear to fear, successively betrayed' –
By making risks to give a cause for fear
(Feeling safe with causes, and from birth afraid),

By climbing higher not to look down, by mere
Destruction of the accustomed because strange
(Too complex a loved system, or too clear),

By needing change but not too great a change
And therefore a new fear – man has achieved
All the advantage of a wider range,

Successfully has the first fear deceived,
Thought the wheels run on sleepers. This is not
The law of nature it has been believed.

Increasing power (it has increased a lot)
Embarrasses 'attempted suicides,'
Narrows their margin. Policies that got

'Virility from war' get much besides;
The mind, as well in mining as in gas
War's parallel, now less easily decides

On a good root-confusion to amass
Much safety from irrelevant despair.
Mere change in numbers made the process crass.

We now turn blank eyes for a pattern there
Where first the race of armament was made;
Where a less involute compulsion played.
'For hunger or for love they bite and tear.'

ROY FISHER

The Entertainment of War

I saw the garden where my aunt had died
And her two children and a woman from next door;
It was like a burst pod filled with clay.

A mile away in the night I had heard the bombs
Sing and then burst themselves between cramped houses
With bright soft flashes and sounds like banging doors;

The last of them crushed the four bodies into the ground,
Scattered the shelter, and blasted my uncle's corpse
Over the housetop and into the street beyond.

Now the garden lay stripped and stale; the iron shelter
Spread out its separate petals around a smooth clay saucer,
Small, and so tidy it seemed nobody had ever been there.

When I saw it, the house was blown clean by blast and care:
Relations had already torn out the new fireplaces;
My cousin's pencils lasted me several years.

And in his office notepad that was given me
I found solemn drawings in crayon of blondes without
    dresses.
In his lifetime I had not known him well.

Those were the things I noticed at ten years of age:
Those, and the four hearses outside our house,
The chocolate cakes, and my classmates' half-shocked envy.

But my grandfather went home from the mortuary
And for five years tried to share the noises in his skull,
Then he walked out and lay under a furze-bush to die.

When my father came back from identifying the daughter
He asked us to remind him of her mouth.
We tried. He said 'I think it was the one'.

These were marginal people I had met only rarely
And the end of the whole household meant that no grief was
    seen;
Never have people seemed so absent from their own deaths.

This bloody episode of four whom I could understand better
    dead
Gave me something I needed to keep a long story moving;
I had no pain of it; can find no scar even now.

But had my belief in the fiction not been thus buoyed up
I might, in the sigh and strike of the next night's bombs
Have realised a little what they meant, and for the first time
    been afraid.

FRANCO FORTINI

Italy 1942

Now I realise I love you
Italy and salute you
Inevitable prison.

Not for your sorrowful streets, you cities
Furrowed like human looks
Not for the ashes of passion
Of the churches, not for the voice
Of your remote books.

But rather for these words
Fashioned by common men, that hammer
Their beat behind my brow;
For this suffering, here and now
That enfolds me, a stranger, within you;

And for this language of mine that I declaim
To grave and ardent men who will come one day
Companions free in their resolute grief.
Now it is not even enough to lay
Down my life for your ancient empty name.

Translated from the Italian by Peter Lawson

Marching Orders

And so from this eminence all is quiet
Where we talk for a spell averting our eyes
And the wind in our hair dies down with the dusk.

And so no pathway to clamber down
But the one to the north, the sunless one,
And the boughs of the trees that turned to water.

And so we'll soon have to hold our tongues.
This evening we'll be in the valley below
Where the festive lanterns have all burnt out.

Where a crowd is silent and friends don't greet you.

Translated by Peter Lawson

1944–1947

The war was on, at night panes
of the sideboard rattled with the drone
of the *Liberators* from the west going eastward
or south, towards Italy. Who was I
and you, who were you? It began like that.

Long and grey lay the lake of Zurich
and the trams sky-blue in the snowy air.

Translated by Peter Lawson

Endlösung

Kube, Thilo, Mèngele, Gisler, Salmuth,
Wítiska, Stroop, Strauch, Borman, Haase,
ach! clay shoved in to gag the gullet, ach, the cord,
what crusts of blood under the nails, what gore
in the runnels of the dissecting slab! Our gang
of old high-school mates, now lofty constellations!

Translated by Peter Lawson

[84]

ANDRÉ FRÉNAUD

The Magi

Shall we go forward as fast as the star?
Hasn't the trip lasted long enough?
Shall we manage to mislead it in the end,
that star amid the moon and the animals,
which is not restless?

Snow had woven the lands of the way back
with its flowers melted where memory is lost.
New companions fell in with the troop,
coming out of the trees like woodcutters.
The wandering Jew laboured, mocked for his wounds.
Furs covered the black king sick to death.
The shepherd of hunger is with us,
his blue eyes light up his cloak of peelings
and the furious flock of captive children.

We were to see joy, so we had thought,
the world's joy born in a house nearby.
That was at the start. Now we don't speak.
We were to set free a glittering tomb,
marked with a cross by the torches in the forest.

The land is uncertain, the castles
slip round behind us.
No fires in the tavern hearths. The frontiers
shift at dawn beneath the forbidden blows.
Our palms which have broken the sandstorms
are drilled by the weevil, and I am afraid of the dark.

Those who were waiting for us on the windy road
have grown weary, the chorus is turning against us.
Through the suburbs closed at dawn, the loveless lands,
we go forward, mingled with all and apart
under hope's heavy eyelids.
Fear was panting like an aged nag.
We shall get there too late, the massacre has begun,
the innocents are lying in the grass.
And every day we stir puddles out here.
And the rumble grows hollow, of the unhelped dead
who had put their hope in our diligence.

All the incense has rotted in the ivory caskets
and the gold has curdled our hearts like milk.
The girl has given herself to the soldiers,
whom we kept under the arch, for the sake of her face,
beaming, smiling.

We are lost. We were given false reports.
Ever since the journey started.
There was no road, there is no light.
Only a nugget of gold out of a dream,
which the weight of our downfalls could not swell.
And we go on murmuring against ourselves,
all three as confused as one man
can be with himself.
And the world muses across our march
through the grass of the low places. And they hope,
when we have taken the wrong way.

Astray in the shot threads of time, the harsh meanders
brought to life by the smile of the Child,
knights in pursuit of the fugitive birth
of the future which guides us like a herdsman,

I curse fortune, I should like to go back
to the house and the plane-tree
to drink my own well water untroubled by the moon,
and to live out my days on my still level terraces,
in the unmoving coolness of my shadow.

But I cannot be cured of a mad call.

1941

Translated from the French by Keith Bosley

The Middle of a War

My photograph already looks historic.
The promising youthful face, the matelot's collar,
Say 'This one is remembered for a lyric.
His place and period – nothing could be duller.'

Its position is already indicated –
The son or brother in the album; pained
The expression and the garments dated,
His fate so obviously pre-ordained.

The original turns away; as horrible thoughts,
Loud fluttering aircraft slope above his head
At dusk. The ridiculous empires break like biscuits.

Ah, life has been abandoned by the boats –
Only the trodden island and the dead
Remain, and the once inestimable caskets.

Autumn 1942

Season of rains: the horizon like an illness
Daily retreating and advancing: men
Swarming on aircraft: things that leave their den
And prowl the suburbs: cries in the starlit stillness–

Into the times' confusion such sharp captions
Are swiftly cut, as symbols give themselves
To poets, though the convenient nymphs and elves
They know fall sadly short of their conceptions.

[88]

I see giraffes that lope, half snake, half steed,
A slowed-up film; the soft bright zebra race,
Unreal as rocking horses; and the face –
A solemn mandarin's – of the wildebeest.

And sometimes in the mess the men and their
Pathetic personal trash become detached
From what they move on; and my days are patched
With newspapers about the siege-like war.

Should I be asked to speak the truth, these are
What I should try to explain, and leave unsaid
Our legacy of failure from the dead.
The silent fate of our provincial star.

But what can be explained? The animals
Are what you make of them, are words, are visions,
And they for us are moving in dimensions
Impertinent to use or watch at all.

And of the men there's nothing to be said:
Only events, with which they wrestle, can
Transfigure them or make them other than
Things to be loved or hated and soon dead.

It is the news at which I hesitate,
That glares authentically between the bars
Of style and lies, and holds enough of fears
And history, and is not too remote.

And tells me that the age is thus: chokes back
My private suffering, the ghosts of nature
And of the mind: it says the human features
Are mutilated, have a dreadful lack.

It half convinces me that some great faculty,
Like hands, has been eternally lost and all
Our virtues now are the high and horrible
Ones of a streaming wound which heals in evil.

ROBERT GARIOCH

1941

Stinking of chlorine and sweit, the sweirt recruits
    wi gaspreif battledress frottan at our skin
feet duntan about in great boss suits,
    bash our tackety ballet, out in the sun.

In sicht of us, some civvy amang the trees,
    wi deck-chair, sandals, bottles on the ice,
cooling his bubbly cider, sits at ease,
    and kens that Man was meant for Paradise.
sweirt, unwilling; *duntan*, bumping; *boss*, hollow

Letter from Italy

From large red bugs, a refugee,
I make my bed beneath the sky,
safe from the crawling enemy
though not secure from nimbler flea.
Late summer darkness comes, and now
I see again the homely Plough
and wonder: do you also see
the seven stars as well as I?
And it is good to find a tie
of seven stars from you to me.
Lying on deck, on friendly seas,
I used to watch, with no delight,
new unsuggestive stars that light

the tedious Antipodes.
Now in a hostile land I lie,
but share with you these ancient high
familiar named divinities.
Perimeters have bounded me,
sad rims of desert and of sea,
the famous one around Tobruk,
and now barbed wire, which way I look,
except above – the Pléiades.

DAVID GASCOYNE

Spring MCMXL

London Bridge is falling down, Rome's burnt, and Babylon
The Great is now but dust; and still Spring must
Swing back through Time's continual arc to earth.
Though every land become as a black field
Dunged with the dead, drenched by the dying's blood,
Still must a punctual goddess waken and ascend
The rocky stairs, up into earth's chilled air,
And pass upon her mission through those carrion ranks,
Picking her way among a maze of broken brick
To quicken with her footsteps the short sooty grass between;
While now once more their futile matchwood empires flare
    and blaze
And through the smoke men gaze with bloodshot eyes
At the translucent apparition, clad in trembling nascent
    green,
Of one they can still recognise, though scarcely understand.

Walking at Whitsun
'La fontaine n'a pas tari
Pas plus que l'or de la paille ne s'est terni
Regardons l'abeille
Et ne songeons pas à l'avenir . . .'
                Apollinaire

. . . Then let the cloth across my back grow warm
Beneath such comforting strong rays! new leaf
Flow everywhere, translucently profuse,

And flagrant weed be tall, the banks of lanes
Sprawl dazed with swarming lion-petalled suns
As with largesse of pollen-coloured wealth
The meadows; and across these vibrant lands
Of Summer-afternoon through which I stroll
Let rapidly gold glazes slide and chase
Away such shades as chill the hillside trees
And make remindful mind turn cold . . .

                          The eyes
Of thought stare elsewhere, as though skewer-fixed
To an imagined sky's immense collapse;
Nor can, borne undistracted through this scene
Of festive plant and basking pastorale,
The mind find any calm or light within
The bone walls of the skull; for at its ear
Resound recurrent thunderings of dark
Smoke-towered waves rearing sheer tons to strike
Down through Today's last dyke. Day-long
That far thick roar of fear thuds, on-and-on,
Beneath the floor of sense, and makes
All carefree quodlibet of leaves and larks
And fragile tympani of insects sound
Like Chinese music, mindlessly remote,
Drawing across both sight and thought like gauze
Its unreality's taut haze.

                         But light!
O cleanse with widespread flood of rays the brain's
Oppressively still sickroom, wherein brood
Hot festering obsessions, and absolve
My introspection's mirror of such stains
As blot its true reflection of the world!
Let streams of sweetest air dissolve the blight

And poison of the News, which every hour
Contaminates the ether.

                              I will pass
On far beyond the village, out of sight
Of human habitation for a while
Grass has an everlasting pristine smell.
On high, sublime in his bronze ark, the sun
Goes cruising across seas of silken sky.
In fields atop the hillside, chestnut trees
Display the splendour of their branches piled
With blazing candle burdens. – Such a May
As this might never come again . . .

                              I tread
The white dust of a weed-bright lane; alone
Upon Time-Present's tranquil outmost rim,
Seeing the sunlight through a lens of dread,
While anguish makes the English landscape seem
Inhuman as the jungle, and unreal
Its peace. And meditating as I pace
The afternoon away, upon the smile
(Like that worn by the dead) which Nature wears
In ignorance of our unnatural tears,
From time to time I think: How such a sun
Must glitter on their helmets! How bright-red
Against this sky's clear screen must ruins burn . . .

How sharply their invading steel must shine!

Marshfield, May 1940

CHAIM GRADE

The Miracle

Because everything I build is built on the miracle
that I survive, panic storms me.
When you go away for an hour out of twenty-four,
don't let the emptiness betray too suddenly
that you're only here in my imagination;
because everything I build is built on a marvel,
and when you go away for an hour, that hour becomes
a long drawnout struckdumb century.
I see that my house is made of fog and smoke,
that the water again has overflowed its banks,
and you're only a dream, an invention of mine
that will fade away in separate moments.

Sometimes I cross a street and I ask:
Did I just walk over a covered grave?
For since I've seen marvels on my way,
I see a world of hidden graves.
Sometimes I stand before my house, forgetting
that this is my house, and my heart howls out;
because everything I build is built on a miracle,
and may become topsy-turvy in the flick of an eyelash.
The miracle makes me sick, old-grey and tired,
and only in my memory am I any younger.
Thus I live like a war invalid
with sensations of shot-off fingers.

Translated from the Yiddish by Ruth Whitman

LUBA KRUGMAN GURDUS

Majdanek

All lost its shape in the dense fog
Save the dimly lit, snowy track
Lined with armed towers, looming high
And search lights, neatly spaced apart

Of the twelve fields we quickly passed
Only one betrayed a feverish rush
With inmates pushing heavy carts
Loaded with corpses, probably gassed

Our truck stopped at gate thirteen
With sentry boxes at opposite ends
Guarding a huge field of unblemished white
Surrounded by a high voltage fence

Along the field small houses in rows
Like entrenched medieval forts
With narrow windows, adorned by frost
And snow-sprinkled wide opened doors

Inside the empty barracks, offensive smells
Mixed with a strong carbolic scent
Attacking nostrils, eyes and throats
With dense and heavy fetoric stench

The barracks seemed emptied in stride
On its three-levelled wooden bunks
Remnants of inmates' gloves and shawls
Traces of violence and fight

Inside the barracks bitter cold
Outside, Majdanek in its glory,
Covered by blankets of snowy white
Under a sapphire, star-studded sky

Translated from the Polish by the author

TONY HARRISON

Sonnets for August 1945: The Morning After

I

The fire left to itself might smoulder weeks.
Phone cables melt. Paint peels from off back gates.
Kitchen windows crack; the whole street reeks
of horsehair blazing. Still it celebrates.

Though people weep, their tears dry from the heat.
Faces flush with flame, beer, sheer relief
and such a sense of celebration in our street
for me it still means joy though banked with grief.

And that, now clouded, sense of public joy
with war-worn adults wild in their loud fling
has never come again since as a boy
I saw Leeds people dance and heard them sing.

There's still that dark, scorched circle on the road.
The morning after kids like me helped spray
hissing upholstery spring wire that still glowed
and cobbles boiling with black gas tar for VJ.

II

The Rising Sun was blackened on those flames.
The jabbering tongues of fire consumed its rays.
Hiroshima, Nagasaki were mere names
for us small boys who gloried in our blaze.

The blood-red ball, first burnt to blackout shreds,
took hovering batwing on the bonfire's heat

above the *Rule Britannias* and the bobbing heads
of the VJ hokey-cokey in our street.

The kitchen blackout cloth became a cloak
for me to play at fiend Count Dracula in.
I swirled it near the fire. It filled with smoke.
Heinz ketchup dribbled down my vampire's chin.

That circle of scorched cobbles scarred with tar 's
a night-sky globe nerve-rackingly all black,
both hemispheres entire but with no stars,
an Archerless zilch, a Scaleless zodiac.

H.D.

from The Walls Do Not Fall
  To Bryher

  for Karnak 1923
  from London 1942

An incident here and there,
and rails gone (for guns)
from your (and my) old town square:

mist and mist-grey, no colour,
still the Luxor bee, chick and hare
pursue unalterable purpose

in green, rose-red, lapis;
they continue to prophesy
from the stone papyrus:

there, as here, ruin opens
the tomb, the temple; enter,
there as here, there are no doors:

the shrine lies open to the sky,
the rain falls, here, there
sand drifts; eternity endures:

ruin everywhere, yet as the fallen roof
leaves the sealed room
open to the air,

so, through our desolation,
thoughts stir, inspiration stalks us
through gloom:

unaware, Spirit announces the Presence;
shivering overtakes us,
as of old, Samuel:

trembling at a known street-corner,
we know not nor are known;
the Pythian pronounces – we pass on

to another cellar, to another sliced wall
where poor utensils show
like rare objects in a museum;

Pompeii has nothing to teach us,
we know crack of volcanic fissure,
slow flow of terrible lava,

pressure on heart, lungs, the brain
about to burst its brittle case
(what the skull can endure!):

over us, Apocryphal fire,
under us, the earth sway, dip of a floor,
slope of a pavement

where men roll, drunk
with a new bewilderment,
sorcery, bedevilment:

the bone-frame was made for
no such shock knit within terror,
yet the skeleton stood up to it:

the flesh? it was melted away,
the heart burnt out, dead ember,
tendons, muscles shattered, outer husk dismembered,

yet the frame held:
we passed the flame: we wonder
what saved us? what for?

ANTHONY HECHT

The Book of Yolek

Wir Haben ein Gesetz,
Und nach dem Gesetz soll er sterben. *

The dowsed coals fume and hiss after your meal
Of grilled brook trout, and you saunter off for a walk
Down the fern trail. It doesn't matter where to,
Just so you're weeks and worlds away from home,
And among midsummer hills have set up camp
In the deep bronze glories of declining day.

You remember, peacefully, an earlier day
In childhood, remember a quite specific meal:
A corn roast and bonfire in summer camp.
That summer you got lost on a Nature Walk;
More than you dared admit, you thought of home:
No one else knows where the mind wanders to.

The fifth of August, 1942.
It was the morning and very hot. It was the day
They came at dawn with rifles to The Home
For Jewish Children, cutting short the meal
Of bread and soup, lining them up to walk
In close formation off to a special camp.

How often you have thought about that camp,
As though in some strange way you were driven to,
And about the children, and how they were made to walk,
Yolek who had bad lungs, who wasn't a day
Over five years old, commanded to leave his meal
And shamble between armed guards to his long home.

We're approaching August again. It will drive home
The regulation torments of that camp
Yolek was sent to, his small, unfinished meal,
The electric fences, the numeral tattoo,
The quite extraordinary heat of the day
They all were forced to take that terrible walk.

Whether on a silent, solitary walk
Or among crowds, far off or safe at home,
You will remember, helplessly, that day,
And the smell of smoke, and the loudspeakers of the camp.
Wherever you are, Yolek will be there, too.
His unuttered name will interrupt your meal.

Prepare to receive him in your home some day.
Though they killed him in the camp they sent him to,
He will walk in as you're sitting down to a meal.

* We have a law, and according to the law he must die.

HAMISH HENDERSON

First Elegy: End of a Campaign

There are many dead in the brutish desert,
        who lie uneasy
among the scrub in this landscape of half-wit
stunted ill-will. For the dead land is insatiate
and necrophilous. The sand is blowing about still.
Many who for various reasons, or because
        of mere unanswerable compulsion, came here
and fought among the clutching gravestones,
        shivered and sweated,
cried out, suffered thirst, were stoically silent, cursed
the spittering machine-guns, were homesick for Europe
and fast embedded in quicksand of Africa
        agonised and died.
And sleep now. Sleep here the sleep of the dust.

There were our own, there were the others.
Their deaths were like their lives, human and animal.
There were no gods and precious few heroes.
What they regretted when they died had nothing to do with
        race and leader, realm indivisible,
laboured Augustan speeches or vague imperial heritage.
(They saw through that guff before the axe fell.)
        Their longing turned to
the lost world glimpsed in the memory of letters:
an evening at the pictures in the friendly dark,
two knowing conspirators smiling and whispering secrets; or
    else
a family gathering in the homely kitchen

with Mum so proud of her boys in uniform:
          their thoughts trembled
between moments of estrangement, and ecstatic moments
of reconciliation: and their desire
crucified itself against the unutterable shadow of someone
whose photo was in their wallets.
Then death made his incision.

There were our own, there were the others.
Therefore, minding the great word of Glencoe's
son, that we should not disfigure ourselves
with villainy of hatred; and seeing that all
have gone down like curs into anonymous silence,
I will bear witness for I knew the others.
Seeing that littoral and interior are alike indifferent
and the birds are drawn again to our welcoming north
why should I not sing *them*, the dead, the innocent?

Third Elegy: Leaving the City

MORNING AFTER. Get moving. Cheerio. Be seeing you
when this party's over. Right, driver, get weaving.

The truck pulls out
along the corniche. We dismiss with the terseness
of a newsreel the casino and the column,
the scrofulous sellers of obscenity,
the garries, the girls and the preposterous skyline.

Leave them. And out past the stinking tanneries,
the maritime Greek cafés, the wogs and the nets
drying among seaweed. Through the periphery of the city
itching under flagrant sunshine. Faster. We are nearing
the stretch leading to the salt-lake Mareotis.

Sand now, and dust-choked fig-trees. This is the road
where convoys are ordered to act in case of ambush.
A straight run through now to the coastal sector.
One sudden thought wounds: it's a half-hour or over
since we saw the last skirt. And for a moment we regret
the women, and the harbour with a curve so perfect
it seems it was drawn with the mouseion's protractor.

Past red-rimmed eye of the salt-lake. So long then,
holy filth of the living. We are going to the familiar
filth of your negation, to rejoin the proletariat
of levelling death. Stripes are shed and ranks levelled
in death's proletariat. There the Colonel of Hussars,
the keen Sapper Subaltern with a first in economics
and the sergeant well known in international football
crouch with Jock and Jame in their holes like helots.
Distinctions become vain, and former privileges quite
    pointless
in that new situation. See our own and the opponents
advance, meet and merge: the commingled columns
lock, strain, disengage and join issue with the dust.

Do not regret
that we have still in history to suffer
or comrade that we are the agents
of a dialectic that can destroy us
but like a man prepared, like a brave man
bid farewell to the city, and quickly
move forward on the road leading west by the salt-lake.
Like a man for long prepared, like a brave man,
like to the man who was worthy of such a city
be glad that the case admits no other solution,
acknowledge with pride the clear imperative of action
and bid farewell to her, to Alexandria, whom you are losing.

[108]

And these, advancing from the direction of Sollum,
swaddies in tropical kit, lifted in familiar vehicles
are they mirage – ourselves out of a mirror?
No, they too, leaving the plateau of Marmarica
for the serpentine of the pass, they advancing towards us
along the coast road, are the others, the brothers
in death's proletariat, they are our victims and betrayers
advancing by the sea-shore to the same assignation.
We send them our greetings out of the mirror.

Interlude: Opening of an Offensive

(A) THE WAITING

Armour has foregathered, snuffling
through tourbillions of fine dust.
The crews don't speak much. They've had
last brew-up before battle. The tawny
deadland lies in a silence
not yet smashed by salvoes.
No sound reaches us
from the African constellations.
The low ridge too is quiet.
But no fear we're sleeping,
no need to remind us
that the nervous fingers of the searchlights
are nearly meeting and time is flickering
and this I think in a few minutes
while the whole power crouches for the spring.
X–20 in thirty seconds. Then begin

(B) THE BARRAGE

Let loose (rounds)
the exultant bounding hell-harrowing of sound.
Break the batteries. Confound
the damnable domination. Slake
the crashing breakers-húrled rúbble of the guns.
Dithering darkness, we'll wake you! Héll's bélls
blind you. Be broken, bleed
deathshead blackness!
                    The thongs of the livid
firelights lick you
                    jagg'd splinters rend you
                                        underground
we'll bomb you, doom you, tomb you into grave's mound

(C) THE JOCKS

They move forward into no man's land, a vibrant sounding
    board.
            As they advance
the guns push further murderous music.
Is this all they will hear, this raucous apocalypse?
The spheres knocking in the night of Heaven?
The drummeling of overwhelming niagara?
No! For I can hear it! Or is it? . . . tell
me that I can hear it! Now – listen!

            Yes, hill and shieling
sea-loch and island, hear it, the yell
of your war-pipes, scaling sound's mountains
guns thunder drowning in their soaring swell!
– The barrage gulfs them: they're gulfed in the clumbering
    guns,

gulfed in gloom, gloom. Dumb in the blunderbuss black –
lost – gone in the anonymous cataract of noise.
Now again! The shrill war-song: it flaunts
aggression to the sullen desert. It mounts. Its scream
tops the valkyrie, tops the colossal
        artillery.

Meaning that many
German Fascists will not be going home
meaning that many
will die, doomed in their false dream

We'll mak siccar!
Against the bashing cudgel
against the contemptuous triumphs of the big battalions
mak siccar against the monkish adepts
of total war against the oppressed oppressors
mak siccar against the leaching lies
against the worked out systems of sick perversion
mak siccar
        against the executioner
against the tyrannous myth and the real terror
mak siccar

Seventh Elegy: Seven Good Germans

*The track running between Mekili and Tmimi was at one time a
kind of no-man's-land. British patrolling was energetic, and there
were numerous brushes with German and Italian elements. El
Eleba lies about half-way along this track.*

Of the swaddies
who came to the desert with Rommel
there were few who had heard (or would hear) of El Eleba.

They recce'd,
             or acted as medical orderlies
or patched up their tanks in the camouflaged workshops
and never gave a thought to a place like El Eleba.

To get there, you drive into the blue, take a bearing
and head for damn-all. Then you're there. And where are
    you?

– Still, of some few who did cross our path at El Eleba
there are seven who bide under their standing crosses.

The first a Lieutenant.
                    When the medicos passed him
for service overseas, he had jotted in a note-book
to the day and the hour keep me steadfast there is only
the decision and the will

                    the rest has no importance

The second a Corporal.
                    He had been in the Legion
and had got one more chance to redeem his lost honour.
What he said was

                    Listen here, I'm fed up with your griping –
If you want extra rations, go get 'em from Tommy!
You're green, that's your trouble. Dodge the column, pass
    the buck
and scrounge all you can – that's our law in the Legion.
You know Tommy's got 'em. . . . He's got mineral waters,
and beer, and fresh fruit in that white crinkly paper
and God knows what all! Well, what's holding you back?
Are you windy or what?

                    Christ, you 'old Afrikaners'!
If you're wanting the eats, go and get 'em from Tommy!

The third had been a farm-hand in the March of Silesia
and had come to the desert as fresh fodder for machine-
     guns.
His dates are inscribed on the files, and on the cross-piece.

The fourth was a lance-jack.
                         He had trusted in Adolf
while working as a chemist in the suburb of Spandau.
His loves were his 'cello, and the woman who had borne
     him
two daughters and a son. He had faith in the Endsieg.
THAT THE NEW REICH MAY LIVE prayed the flyleaf of his
     Bible.

The fifth a mechanic.
                         All the honour and glory,
the siege of Tobruk and the conquest of Cairo
meant as much to that Boche as the Synod of Whitby.
Being wise to all this, he had one single headache,
which was, how to get back to his sweetheart (called Ilse).
– He had said
          Can't the Tommy wake up and get weaving?
If he tried, he could put our whole Corps in the bag.
May God damn this Libya and both of its palm-trees!

The sixth was a Pole
                         – or to you, a Volksdeutscher–
who had put off his nation to serve in the Wehrmacht.
He siegheiled, and talked of 'the dirty Polacken',
and said what he'd do if let loose among Russkis.
His mates thought that, though 'just a polnischer Schwein-
     hund',
he was not a bad bloke.
                         On the morning concerned

he was driving a truck with mail, petrol and rations.
The M.P. on duty shouted five words of warning.
He nodded
        laughed
              revved
                     and drove straight for El Eleba
not having quite got the chap's Styrian lingo.

The seventh a young swaddy.
                     Riding cramped in a lorry
to death along the road which winds eastward to Halfaya
he had written three verses in appeal against his sentence
which soften for an hour the anger of Lenin.
        Seven poor bastards
        dead in African deadland
   (tawny tousled hair under the issue blanket)
          wie einst Lili
        dead in African deadland

                  einst Lili Marleen

ZBIGNIEW HERBERT

Why the Classics
(for A.H.)

1

in the fourth book of *The Peloponnesian War*
Thucydides describes his unsuccessful expedition

amid long speeches by generals
sieges battles disease
thick webs of intrigue
diplomatic démarches
that episode is like a needle
in a forest

the Athenian colony Amphipolis
fell to Brasydas
because Thucydides' relief was late

for this he paid with life-long exile
from his native city

exiles of all time
know that price

2

the generals in recent wars
in similar predicaments
yap on their knees before posterity
praise their own heroism
and innocence

they blame subordinates
envious colleagues
and hostile winds

Thucydides merely says
it was winter
he had seven ships
had sailed at speed

3

should the theme of art
be a broken jug
a tiny broken soul
full of self-pity

then what shall remain of us
will be like lovers' tears
in a dingy small hotel
when wallpapers dawn

Translated from the Polish by John and Bogdana Carpenter

The Rain

When my older brother
came back from war
he had on his forehead a little silver star
and under the star
an abyss

a splinter of shrapnel
hit him at Verdun
or perhaps at Grünwald
(he'd forgotten the details)

he used to talk much
in many languages
but he liked most of all
the language of history

until losing breath
he commanded his dead pals to run
Roland Kowalski Hannibal

he shouted
that this was the last crusade
that Carthage soon would fall
and then sobbing confessed
that Napoleon did not like him

we looked at him
getting paler and paler
abandoned by his senses
he turned slowly into a monument

into musical shells of ears
entered a stone forest

and the skin of his face
was secured
with the blind dry
buttons of eyes

nothing was left him
but touch

what stories
he told with his hands
in the right he had romances
in the left soldier's memories

they took my brother
and carried him out of town

he returns every fall
slim and very quiet
he does not want to come in
he knocks at the window for me

we walk together in the streets
and he recites to me
improbable tales
touching my face
with blind fingers of rain

Translated by John and Bogdana Carpenter

GEOFFREY HILL

September Song
born 19.6.32 – deported 24.9.42

Undesirable you may have been, untouchable
you were not. Not forgotten
or passed over at the proper time.

As estimated, you died. Things marched,
sufficient, to that end.
Just so much Zyklon and leather, patented
terror, so many routine cries.

(I have made
an elegy for myself it
is true)

September fattens on vines. Roses
flake from the wall. The smoke
of harmless fires drifts to my eyes.

This is plenty. This is more than enough.

MIROSLAV HOLUB

Five Minutes after the Air Raid

In Pilsen,
twenty-six Station Road,
she climbed to the third floor
up stairs which were all that was left
of the whole house,
she opened her door
full on to the sky,
stood gaping over the edge.

For this was the place
the world ended.

Then
she locked up carefully
lest someone steal
Sirius
or Aldebaran
from her kitchen,
went back downstairs
and settled herself
to wait
for the house to rise again
and for her husband to rise from the ashes
and for her children's hands and feet to be stuck back in
    place.

In the morning they found her
still as stone,
sparrows pecking her hands.

Translated from the Czech by George Theiner

The Fly

She sat on a willow trunk
watching
part of the battle of Crécy,
the shouts,
the gasps,
the groans,
the tramping and the tumbling.

During the fourteenth charge
of the French cavalry
she mated
with a brown-eyed male fly
from Vadincourt.

She rubbed her legs together
as she sat on a disembowelled horse
meditating
on the immortality of flies.

With relief she alighted
on the blue tongue
of the Duke of Clervaux.

When silence settled
and only the whisper of decay
softly circled the bodies

and only
a few arms and legs
still twitched jerkily under the trees,

she began to lay her eggs
on the single eye

of Johann Uhr,
the Royal Armourer.

And thus it was
that she was eaten by a swift
fleeing
from the fires of Estrées.

Translated by George Theiner

PETER HUCHEL

Wei Dun and the Old Masters

Marvelling at the old masters,
Who painted boulders as bones of the earth
And thin mists as the skin of hills,
I had tried, with vertical brush,
With quick strokes and slow ones,
To colour the moist radiance of rain.

But as moon and sun shone
On land going more and more to ruin
It was not boulders that were the earth's bones –
Human bones were grinding in the sand
Where tanks ripped with guzzling tracks
Roads open to their grey marrow.

Old masters, I scraped the paint block,
I cleaned the brush of goat hair.
Yet as I rambled behind the foe
I saw the meadows waterless,
The mill wheel shattered, in hardened gear
The oxen hang rigid in the whim-shaft,
The temple porch plundered
Where on glazed tiles in a heap
The snake dozed all the white noon.

Old masters, how can I paint
The river's rocky dorsal fins
As if, in the shallows, there was lurking
Some giant fish with gills of sun.
And paint the cool bloom of the mist,

The grey whiteness of buoyant snowy air,
As if soft feathers floated from a windy nest.

Where, where have they gone, your heavens,
Into what distances, exalted masters,
The breath of the world, so vulnerable?
Images of terror visited me
And etched my eye with smoke and sorrow.
Where have you gone, Boatman Playing the Flute?
Do you watch in the rain the wild geese flying?
Over the river at night a moaning went.
Your wife with a smoking branch raked
Ashes and embers of your bamboo hut,
To discover there your blackened skull.

And Old Man Going Home from a Village Feast,
Quietly riding your water buffalo,
Through the coolness of falling dew,
Didn't your servant stop in horror
And let the rope loosely hang down?
You rode the buffalo behind the cliff.
By then the foe was at your door.

Where is the Farm by the Lake, fanned
By a chevelure of trees and grasses?
And where in the snow, filtered through mist,
The lonely Village in the High Mountains?
Search behind the penfold of the fire.
War has baked all things dry
In this kiln of death.

Where are the voices, noise of gongs,
The odour of pigment, you poets and painters
Of the Landscape Populated by Scholars?
Dumb, on the level field, how you lie,

Robbed of your shoes, your amulets,
Abandoned to the birds and winds.

Heaven and Earth sustain
Still the ten thousand things.
Deep down, the bones rot.
But the breath flies upward,
Flowing as light you walked through once,
Old masters, with great composure.

Translated from the German by Michael Hamburger

Roads

Choked sunset glow
Of crashing time.
Roads. Roads.
Intersections of flight.
Cart tracks across the ploughed field
That with the eyes
Of killed horses
Saw the sky in flames.

Nights with lungs full of smoke,
With the hard breath of the fleeing
When shots
Struck the dusk.
Out of a broken gate
Ash and wind came without a sound,
A fire
That sullenly chewed the darkness.

Corpses,
Flung over the rail tracks,

Their stifled cry
Like a stone on the palate.
A black
Humming cloth of flies
Closed their wounds.

Translated by Michael Hamburger

RANDALL JARRELL

The Death of the Ball Turret Gunner

From my mother's sleep I fell into the State,
And I hunched in its belly till my wet fur froze.
Six miles from earth, loosed from its dream of life,
I woke to black flak and the nightmare fighters.
When I died they washed me out of the turret with a hose.

Eighth Air Force

If, in an odd angle of the hutment,
A puppy laps the water from a can
Of flowers, and the drunk sergeant shaving
Whistles *O Paradiso!* – shall I say that man
Is not as men have said: a wolf to man?

The other murderers troop in yawning;
Three of them play Pitch, one sleeps, and one
Lies counting missions, lies there sweating
Till even his heart beats: One; One; One.
O murderers! . . . Still, this is how it's done:

This is a war. . . . But since these play, before they die,
Like puppies with their puppy; since, a man,
I did as these have done, but did not die –
I will content the people as I can
And give up these to them: Behold the man!

I have suffered, in a dream, because of him,
Many things; for this last saviour, man,

I have lied as I lie now. But what is lying?
Men wash their hands, in blood, as best they can:
I find no fault in this just man.

Losses

It was not dying: everybody died.
It was not dying: we had died before
In the routine crashes – and our fields
Called up the papers, wrote home to our folks,
And the rates rose, all because of us.
We died on the wrong page of the almanac,
Scattered on mountains fifty miles away;
Diving on haystacks, fighting with a friend,
We blazed up on the lines we never saw.
We died like aunts or pets or foreigners.
(When we left high school nothing else had died
For us to figure we had died like.)

In our new planes, with our new crews, we bombed
The ranges by the desert or the shore,
Fired at towed targets, waited for our scores –
And turned into replacements and woke up
One morning, over England, operational.
It wasn't different: but if we died
It was not an accident but a mistake
(But an easy one for anyone to make).
We read our mail and counted up our missions –
In bombers named for girls, we burned
The cities we had learned about in school –
Till our lives wore out; our bodies lay among
The people we had killed and never seen.

When we lasted long enough they gave us medals;
When we died they said, 'Our casualties were low.'
They said, 'Here are the maps'; we burned the cities.

It was not dying – no, not ever dying;
But the night I died I dreamed that I was dead,
And the cities said to me: 'Why are you dying?
We are satisfied, if you are; but why did I die?'

Jews at Haifa

The freighter, gay with rust,
Coasts to a bare wharf of the harbor.
From the funnel's shade (the arbor
Of gourds from which the prophet, without trust,
Watched his old enemies,
The beings of this earth) I scrutinise

The hundreds at the rail
Lapped in the blue blaze of this sea
Who stare till their looks fail
At the earth that they are promised; silently
See the sand-bagged machine-guns,
The red-kneed soldiers blinking in the sun.

A machine-gun away
Are men with our faces: we are torn
With the live blaze of day –
Till we feel shifting, wrenched apart, the worn
Named stones of our last knowledge:
That all men wish our death. Here on the edge

Of the graves of Europe
We believe: truly, we are not dead;

It seems to us that hope
Is possible – that even mercy is permitted
To men on this earth,
To Jews on this earth. . . . But at Cyprus, the red earth,

The huts, the trembling wire
That wreathes us, are to us familiar
As death. All night, the fires
Float their sparks up to the yellow stars;
From the steel, stilted tower
The light sweeps over us. We whisper: 'Ours.'

Ours; and the stones slide home.
There is no hope; 'in all this world
There is no other wisdom
Than ours: we have understood the world,'
We think; but hope, in dread
Search for one doubt, and whisper: 'Truly, we are not dead.'

Prisoners

Within the wires of the post, unloading the cans of garbage,
The three in soiled blue denim (the white *P* on their backs
Sending its chilly *North* six yards to the turning blackened
Sights of the cradled rifle, to the eyes of the yawning guard)
Go on all day being punished, go on all month, all year
Loading, unloading; give their child's, beast's sigh – of
    despair,
Of endurance and of existence; look unexpectingly
At the big guard, dark in his khaki, at the dust of the blazing
    plain,
At the running or crawling soldiers in their soiled and
    shapeless green.

The prisoners, the guards, the soldiers – they are all, in their
    way, being trained.
From these moments, repeated forever, our own new world
    will be made.

A Lullaby

For wars his life and half a world away
The soldier sells his family and days.
He learns to fight for freedom and the State;
He sleeps with seven men within six feet.

He picks up matches and he cleans out plates;
Is lied to like a child, cursed like a beast.
They crop his head, his dog tags ring like sheep
As his stiff limbs shift wearily to sleep.

Recalled in dreams or letters, else forgot,
His life is smothered like a grave, with dirt;
And his dull torment mottles like a fly's
The lying amber of the histories.

Mail Call

The letters always just evade the hand.
One skates like a stone into a beam, falls like a bird.
Surely the past from which the letters rise
Is waiting in the future, past the graves?
The soldiers are all haunted by their lives.

Their claims upon their kind are paid in paper
That establishes a presence, like a smell.

In letters and in dreams they see the world.
They are waiting: and the years contract
To an empty hand, to one unuttered sound –

The soldier simply wishes for his name.

MITSUHARU KANEKO

Ascension

Today is execution day for the pacifists.
Escaping from the gunfire as their corpses topple,
Their souls have ascended to heaven.
To proclaim injustice and iniquity.

In grief, their spirits have begun to relent,
Calling from the edge
Of a great four-cornered ice-floe,
Turning to a rainbow flickering in the dark.

Bombs have exploded; fireworks have crackled:
Their souls, sent drifting to one corner of heaven,
Turned into mist, into spume, into cloud-drifts,
To stain the sky with blood that is still hot.

*Translated from the Japanese by Geoffrey Bownas
and Anthony Thwaite*

Nerves
(Sept. 2nd, 1939)

I think I'll get a paper,
I think I'd better wait.
I'll hear the news at six o'clock,
That's much more up to date.

It's just like last September,
Absurd how time stands still;
They're bound to make a statement.
I don't suppose they will.

I think I'd better stroll around.
Perhaps it's best to stay.
I think I'll have a whisky neat,
I can't this time of day.

I think I'll have another smoke.
I don't know what to do.
I promised to ring someone up,
I can't remember who.

They say it's been averted.
They say we're on the brink.
I'll wait for the 'New Statesman',
I wonder what they think.

They're shouting. It's a Special.
It's not. It's just street cries.
I think the heat is frightful.
God damn these bloody flies.

I see the nation's keeping cool,
The public calm is fine.
This crisis can't shake England's nerves.
It's playing hell with mine.

The Passionate Profiteer to his Love
(After Christopher Marlowe)

Come feed with me and be my love,
And pleasures of the table prove,
Where *Prunier* and *The Ivy* yield
Choice dainties of the stream and field.

At *Claridge* thou shalt duckling eat,
Sip vintages both dry and sweet,
And thou shalt squeeze between thy lips
Asparagus with buttered tips.

On caviare my love shall graze,
And plump on salmon mayonnaise,
And browse at *Scott*'s beside thy swain
On lobster Newburg with champagne.

Between hors d'oeuvres and canapés
I'll feast thee on *poularde soufflé*
And every day within thy reach
Pile melon, nectarine and peach.

Come share at the *Savoy* with me
The menu of austerity;
If in these pastures thou wouldst rove
Then feed with me and be my love.

SIDNEY KEYES

Europe's Prisoners

Never a day, never a day passes
But I remember them, their stoneblind faces
Beaten by arclights, their eyes turned inward
Seeking an answer and their passage homeward:

For being citizens of time, they never
Would learn the body's nationality.
Tortured for years now, they refuse to sever
Spirit from flesh or accept our callow century.

Not without hope, but lacking present solace,
The preacher knows the feel of nails and grace;
The singer snores; the orator's facile hands
Are fixed in a gesture no one understands.

Others escaped, yet paid for their betrayal:
Even the politicians with their stale
Visions and cheap flirtation with the past
Will not die any easier at the last.

The ones who took to garrets and consumption
In foreign cities, found a deeper dungeon
Than any Dachau. Free but still confined
The human lack of pity split their mind.

Whatever days, whatever seasons pass,
The prisoners must stare in pain's white face:
Until at last the courage they have learned
Shall burst the walls and overturn the world.

21st May 1941

[136]

Medallion

Bull-chested and iron-eyed heroes
And weeping women
Surround me while I sleep;
Waking, I meet the continual procession
Of hawk-headed, bird-clawed women
And weeping men.

March 1942

War Poet

I am the man who looked for peace and found
My own eyes barbed.
I am the man who groped for words and found
An arrow in my hand.
I am the builder whose firm walls surround
A slipping land.
When I grow sick or mad
Mock me not nor chain me:
When I reach for the wind
Cast me not down:
Though my face is a burnt book
And a wasted town.

March 1942

RACHEL KORN

My Mother Often Wept

A birch tree may be growing on the mound
heaped by a murderer's hands
in thick woods near the town of Greyding,
and only a bird goes there to honour the dead

where my mother lies in an unknown grave,
a German bullet in her heart.
And I go, go, go there only in dreams,
my eyes shut, my mouth dumb.

I remember that my mother often wept,
and I, I imagined
Abraham's son, bound for the sacrifice, looking to her
from the pages of her prayerbook
while she lived Sarah's fate

and we tumbled, laughed, and played,
despite our father's early death –
Had he lived, our good father,
he would never, never
have taken us to Mount Moriah to be sacrificed.

And yet my mother wept so often –
Did she know
that heaven had prepared
to open wide its gates
and take her sons
in billowing clouds of smoke?

And I was left behind, her only daughter,
like a thorn in dry ground,
and I am the voice of my mother's tears,
I am the sound
of her weeping.

Translated from the Yiddish by Seymour Levitan

GÜNTER KUNERT

On Certain Survivors

When the man
Was dragged out from under
The debris
Of his shelled house,
He shook himself
And said:
Never again.

At least, not right away.

Translated from the German by Michael Hamburger

On the Archaeology of Our Being Buried Alive

Rain, and rain again,
war, and war again
one merciful, one merciless
once, nature at first hand, once
at second hand.

A train runs again
after thirty years of fighting
on the same old line as before,
ruins disappear
but with them, the world
as it had been.

We never really take leave
of our past

because before we come to it
it collapsed
into dust and ashes, somewhere,
when it was still called present.

We would also like to embrace
the dead some time, if they had not been
made into words,
long skeins of words,
which no longer resemble a shape.

Had we been able to keep the voices
of dying, our ears would hardly
be so deafened from talk.
Sometimes things are
impenetrable, sometimes crystal clear
but like pieces of broken glass
before you cut yourself on them
and bleed to death.

Translated by Trude Schwab and Desmond Graham

STANLEY KUNITZ

Reflection by a Mailbox

When I stand in the center of that man's madness,
Deep in his trauma, as in the crater of a wound,
My ancestors step from my American bones.
There's mother in a woven shawl, and that,
No doubt, is father picking up his pack
For the return voyage through those dreadful years
Into the winter of the raging eye.

One generation past, two days by plane away,
My house is dispossessed, my friends dispersed,
My teeth and pride knocked in, my people game
For the hunters of man-skins in the warrens of Europe,
The impossible creatures of an hysteriac's dream
Advancing with hatchets sunk into their skulls
To rip the god out of the machine.

Are these the citizens of the new estate
To which the continental shelves aspire;
Or the powerful get of a dying age, corrupt
And passion-smeared, with fluid on their lips,
As if a soul had been given to petroleum?

How shall we uncreate that lawless energy?

Now I wait under the hemlock by the road
For the red-haired postman with the smiling hand
To bring me my passport to the war.
Familiarly his car shifts into gear
Around the curve; he coasts up to my drive; the day

Strikes noon; I think of Pavlov and his dogs
And the motto carved on the broad lintel of his brain:
'Sequence, consequence, and again consequence.'

PRIMO LEVI

Buna

Torn feet and cursed earth,
The long line in the gray morning.
The Buna smokes from a thousand chimneys,
A day like every other day awaits us.
The whistles terrible at dawn:
'You multitudes with dead faces,
On the monotonous horror of the mud
Another day of suffering is born.'
Tired companion, I see you in my heart.
I read your eyes, sad friend.
In your breast you carry cold, hunger, nothing.
You have broken what's left of the courage within you.
Colorless one, you were a strong man,
A woman walked at your side.
Empty companion who no longer has a name,
Forsaken man who can no longer weep,
So poor you no longer grieve,
So tired you no longer fear.
Spent once-strong man.
If we were to meet again
Up there in the world, sweet beneath the sun,
With what kind of face would we confront each other?

28 December 1945

Translated from the Italian by Ruth Feldman and Brian Swann

Shemà

You who live secure
In your warm houses,
Who return at evening to find
Hot food and friendly faces:

Consider whether this is a man,
Who labors in the mud
Who knows no peace
Who fights for a crust of bread
Who dies at a yes or a no.
Consider whether this is a woman,
Without hair or name
With no more strength to remember
Eyes empty and womb cold
As a frog in winter.

Consider that this has been:
I commend these words to you.
Engrave them on your hearts
When you are in your house, when you walk on your way,
When you go to bed, when you rise.
Repeat them to your children.
Or may your house crumble,
Disease render you powerless,
Your offspring avert their faces from you.

10 January 1946

Translated by Ruth Feldman and Brian Swann

For Adolf Eichmann

The wind runs free across our plains,
The live sea beats for ever at our beaches.
Man makes earth fertile, earth gives him flowers and fruits.
He lives in toil and joy; he hopes, fears, begets sweet
    offspring.

. . . And you have come, our precious enemy,
Forsaken creature, man ringed by death.
What can you say now, before our assembly?
Will you swear by a god? What god?
Will you leap happily into the grave?
Or will you at the end, like the industrious man
Whose life was too brief for his long art,
Lament your sorry work unfinished,
The thirteen million still alive?

Oh son of death, we do not wish you death.
May you live longer than anyone ever lived.
May you live sleepless five million nights,
And may you be visited each night by the suffering of
    everyone who saw,
Shutting behind him, the door that blocked the way back,
Saw it grow dark around him, the air fill with death.

20 July 1960

Translated by Ruth Feldman and Brian Swann

The Girl-Child of Pompei

Since everyone's anguish is our own,
We live yours over again, thin child,

[146]

Clutching your mother convulsively
As though, when the noon sky turned black,
You wanted to re-enter her.
To no avail, because the air, turned poison,
Filtered to find you through the closed windows
Of your quiet thick-walled house,
Once happy with your song, your timid laugh.
Centuries have passed, the ash has petrified
To imprison those delicate limbs for ever.
In this way you stay with us, a twisted plaster cast,
Agony without end, terrible witness to how much
Our proud seed matters to the gods.
Nothing is left of your far-removed sister,
The Dutch girl imprisoned by four walls
Who wrote of her youth without tomorrows.
Her silent ash was scattered by the wind,
Her brief life shut into a crumpled notebook.
Nothing remains of the Hiroshima schoolgirl,
A shadow printed on a wall by the light of a thousand suns,
Victim sacrificed on the altar of fear.
Powerful of the earth, masters of new poisons,
Sad secret guardians of final thunder,
The torments heaven sends us are enough.
Before your finger presses down, stop and consider.

20 November 1978

Translated by Ruth Feldman and Brian Swann

The Survivor

to B.V.

Dopo di allora, ad ora incerta,
Since then, at an uncertain hour,
That agony returns:
And till my ghastly tale is told,
This heart within me burns.

Once more he sees his companions' faces
Livid in the first faint light,
Grey with cement dust,
Nebulous in the mist,
Tinged with death in their uneasy sleep.
At night, under the heavy burden
Of their dreams, their jaws move,
Chewing a nonexistent turnip.
'Stand back, leave me alone, submerged people,
Go away. I haven't dispossessed anyone,
Haven't usurped anyone's bread.
No one died in my place. No one.
Go back into your mist.
It's not my fault if I live and breathe,
Eat, drink, sleep and put on clothes.'

4 February 1984

Translated by Ruth Feldman and Brian Swann

ALUN LEWIS

Raiders' Dawn

Softly the civilised
Centuries fall,
Paper on paper,
Peter on Paul.

And lovers waking
From the night –
Eternity's masters,
Slaves of Time –
Recognise only
The drifting white
Fall of small faces
In pits of lime.

Blue necklace left
On a charred chair
Tells that Beauty
Was startled there.

All Day It Has Rained

All day it has rained, and we on the edge of the moors
Have sprawled in our bell-tents, moody and dull as boors,
Groundsheets and blankets spread on the muddy ground
And from the first grey wakening we have found
No refuge from the skirmishing fine rain
And the wind that made the canvas heave and flap
And the taut wet guy-ropes ravel out and snap.

All day the rain has glided, wave and mist and dream,
Drenching the gorse and heather, a gossamer stream
Too light to stir the acorns that suddenly
Snatched from their cups by the wild south-westerly
Pattered against the tent and our upturned dreaming faces.
And we stretched out, unbuttoning our braces,
Smoking a Woodbine, darning dirty socks,
Reading the Sunday papers – I saw a fox
And mentioned it in the note I scribbled home; –
And we talked of girls, and dropping bombs on Rome,
And thought of the quiet dead and the loud celebrities
Exhorting us to slaughter, and the herded refugees;
– Yet thought softly, morosely of them, and as indifferently
As of ourselves or those whom we
For years have loved, and will again
Tomorrow maybe love; but now it is the rain
Possesses us entirely, the twilight and the rain.

And I can remember nothing dearer or more to my heart
Than the children I watched in the woods on Saturday
Shaking down burning chestnuts for the schoolyard's merry
    play,
Or the shaggy patient dog who followed me
By Sheet and Steep and up the wooded scree
To the Shoulder O' Mutton where Edward Thomas brooded
    long
On death and beauty – till a bullet stopped his song.

A Troopship in the Tropics

Five thousand souls are here and all are bounded
Too easily perhaps by the ostensible purpose,

Steady as the ploughshare cleaving England,
Of this great ship, obedient to its compass.

The sundeck for the children and the officers
Under the awning, watching the midsea blue
Until the nurses pass with a soft excitement
Rustling the talk of passengers and crew.

Deep in the foetid holds the tiered bunks
Hold restless men who sweat and toss and sob;
The gamblers on the hatches, in the corner
The accordionist and barber do their job.

The smell of oranges and excrement
Moves among those who write uneasy letters
Or slouch about and curse the stray dejection
That chafes them with its hard nostalgic fetters.

But everywhere in this sweltering Utopia,
In the bareheaded crowd's two minutes' silence,
In corners where the shadows lie like water,
Are tranquil pools of crystal-clear reflexion.

Time is no mystery now; this torrid blueness
Blazed in a fortnight from the English winter.
Distance is subject to our moods and wishes.
Only the void of feeling must be filled.

And as the ship makes peace within herself
The simple donors of goodness with rugged features
Move in the crowd and share their crusts of wisdom;
Life does not name her rough undoctored teachers.

Welsh songs surge softly in the circling darkness;
Thoughts sail back like swans to the English winter;
Strange desires drift into the mind;
Time hardens. But the ruthless Now grows kind.

The Assault Convoy

Three days of waiting in the islands
Of a remote inhospitable bay
Have soured the small dry stretch of time
Which we allow to drift away
Disconsolate that death should so delay

His wild and breathless act upon the fore-shore
The seas still separate and hide.
Our hobnails stamp in crazy repetition,
Bodies' sweat to bodies' sweat confide
The intimacy we denied.

The nihilist persistence of the sun,
The engines throbbing heatedly all night,
The white refineries of salt and dust
Forbid the mind to think, the pen to write;
We trample down the fences of delight.

Perhaps the ultimate configuration
Of island and peninsula and reef
Will have the same shapes, tortuous and crannied
And the same meaning as our dark belief,
The solid contours of our native grief.

The real always fades into the meaning,
From cone to thread some grave perception drives
The twisted failures into vast fulfilments.
After the holocaust of shells and knives,
The victory, the treaty, the betrayal,
The supersession of a million lives,
The hawk sees something stir among the trenches,
The field mouse hears the sigh of what survives.

The Mahratta Ghats

The valleys crack and burn, the exhausted plains
Sink their black teeth into the horny veins
Straggling the hills' red thighs, the bleating goats
– Dry bents and bitter thistles in their throats –
Thread the loose rocks by immemorial tracks.
Dark peasants drag the sun upon their backs.

High on the ghat the new turned soil is red,
The sun has ground it to the finest red,
It lies like gold within each horny hand.
Siva has spilt his seed upon this land.

Will she who burns and withers on the plain
Leave, ere too late, her scraggy herds of pain,
The cow-dung fire and the trembling beasts,
The little wicked gods, the grinning priests,
And climb, before a thousand years have fled,
High as the eagle to her mountain bed
Whose soil is fine as flour and blood-red?

But no! She cannot move. Each arid patch
Owns the lean folk who plough and scythe and thatch
Its grudging yield and scratch its stubborn stones.
The small gods suck the marrow from their bones.

Who is it climbs the summit of the road?
Only the beggar bumming his dark load.
Who was it cried to see the falling star?
Only the landless soldier lost in war.

And did a thousand years go by in vain?
And does another thousand start again?

C. DAY LEWIS

Where are the War Poets?

They who in folly or mere greed
Enslaved religion, markets, laws,
Borrow our language now and bid
Us to speak up in freedom's cause.

It is the logic of our times,
No subject for immortal verse –
That we who lived by honest dreams
Defend the bad against the worse.

If I go up to yonder town

I went down to yonder town
with the sentence of my death in my hand.
I myself wrote it on my heart
as ransom for my darling's state:
I was going to a war
and she was bruised and wretched
with no lover in the wide world
who would care for what she had of grace.

I went down to yonder town
with the sentence of my death in my hand
written with two wrongs:
the great wrong of the Nazis
and the great wrong of her misery:
two wrongs that were agreeing
that I should stay on the battlefield
since my own girl was exposed
to a pain for which beauty is no respite.

Translated from the Gaelic by the author

Going Westwards

I go westwards in the Desert
with my shame on my shoulders,
that I was made a laughing-stock
since I was as my people were.

Love and the greater error,
deceiving honour spoiled me,
with a film of weakness on my vision,
squinting at mankind's extremity.

Far from me the Island
when the moon rises on Quattara,
far from me the Pine Headland
when the morning ruddiness is on the Desert.

Camus Alba is far from me
and so is the bondage of Europe,
far from me in the North-West
the most beautiful grey-blue eyes.

Far from me the Island
and every loved image in Scotland,
there is a foreign sand in History
spoiling the machines of the mind.

Far from me Belsen and Dachau,
Rotterdam, the Clyde and Prague,
and Dimitrov before a court
hitting fear with the thump of his laugh.

Guernica itself is very far
from the innocent corpses of the Nazis
who are lying in the gravel
and in the khaki sand of the Desert.

There is no rancour in my heart
against the hardy soldiers of the Enemy,
but the kinship that there is among
men in prison on a tidal rock

waiting for the sea flowing
and making cold the warm stone;

and the coldness of life
in the hot sun of the Desert.

But this is the struggle not to be avoided,
the sore extreme of human-kind,
and though I do not hate Rommel's army
the brain's eye is not squinting.

And be what was as it was,
I am of the big men of Braes,
of the heroic Raasay MacLeods,
of the sharp-sword Mathesons of Lochalsh;

and the men of my name – who were braver
when their ruinous pride was kindled?

Translated by the author

Death Valley

Some Nazi or other has said that the Fuehrer had restored to German manhood the 'right and joy of dying in battle'

Sitting dead in 'Death Valley'
below the Ruweisat Ridge
a boy with his forelock down about his cheek
and his face slate-grey;

I thought of the right and the joy
that he got from his Fuehrer,
of falling in the field of slaughter
to rise no more;

of the pomp and the fame
that he had, not alone,
though he was the most piteous to see
in a valley gone to seed

with flies about grey corpses
on a dun sand
dirty yellow and full of the rubbish
and fragments of battle.

Was the boy of the band
who abused the Jews
and Communists, or of the greater
band of those

led, from the beginning of generations,
unwillingly to the trial
and mad delirium of every war
for the sake of rulers?

Whatever his desire or mishap,
his innocence or malignity,
he showed no pleasure in his death
below the Ruweisat Ridge.

Translated by the author

Heroes

I did not see Lannes at Ratisbon
nor MacLennan at Auldearn
nor Gillies MacBain at Culloden,
but I saw an Englishman in Egypt.

A poor little chap with chubby cheeks
and knees grinding each other,
pimply unattractive face –
garment of the bravest spirit.

He was not a hit 'in the pub
in the time of the fists being closed',
but a lion against the breast of battle,
in the morose wounding showers.

His hour came with the shells,
with the notched iron splinters,
in the smoke and flame,
in the shaking and terror of the battlefield.

Word came to him in the bullet shower
that he should be a hero briskly,

and he was that while he lasted
but it wasn't much time he got.

He kept his guns to the tanks,
bucking with tearing crashing screech,
until he himself got, about the stomach,
that biff that put him to the ground,
mouth down in sand and gravel,
without a chirp from his ugly high-pitched voice.

No cross or medal was put to his
chest or to his name or to his family;
there were not many of his troop alive,
and if there were their word would not be strong.
And at any rate, if a battle post stands
many are knocked down because of him,
not expecting fame, not wanting a medal
or any froth from the mouth of the field of slaughter.

I saw a great warrior of England,
a poor manikin on whom no eye would rest;
no Alasdair of Glen Garry;
and he took a little weeping to my eyes.

   Translated by the author

Cushendun

Fuchsia and ragweed and the distant hills
Made as it were out of clouds and sea:
All night the bay is plashing and the moon
   Marks the break of the waves.

Limestone and basalt and a whitewashed house
With passages of great stone flags
And a walled garden with plums on the wall
   And a bird piping in the night.

Forgetfulness: brass lamps and copper jugs
And home-made bread and the smell of turf or flax
And the air a glove and the water lathering easy
   And convolvulus in the hedge.

Only in the dark green room beside the fire
With the curtains drawn against the winds and waves
There is a little box with a well-bred voice:
   What a place to talk of War.

   August–September 1939

Bar-room Matins

Popcorn peanuts clams and gum:
We whose Kingdom has not come
Have mouths like men but still are dumb

Who only deal with Here and Now
As circumstances may allow:
The sponsored programme tells us how.

And yet the preachers tell the pews
What man misuses God can use:
Give us this day our daily news

That we may hear behind the brain
And through the sullen heat's migraine
The atavistic voice of Cain:

'Who entitled you to spy
From your easy heaven? Am I
My brother's keeper? Let him die.'

And God in words we soon forget
Answers through the radio set:
'The curse is on his forehead yet.'

Mass destruction, mass disease:
We thank thee, Lord, upon our knees
That we were born in times like these

When with doom tumbling from the sky
Each of us has an alibi
For doing nothing – Let him die.

Let him die, his death will be
A drop of water in the sea,
A journalist's commodity.

Pretzels crackers chips and beer:
Death is something that we fear
But it titillates the ear.

Anchovy almond ice and gin:
All shall die though none can win;
Let the Untergang begin –

Die the soldiers, die the Jews,
And all the breadless homeless queues.
Give us this day our daily news.

July 1940

Brother Fire

When our brother Fire was having his dog's day
Jumping the London streets with millions of tin cans
Clanking at his tail, we heard some shadow say
'Give the dog a bone' – and so we gave him ours;
Night after night we watched him slaver and crunch away
The beams of human life, the tops of topless towers.

Which gluttony of his for us was Lenten fare
Who mother-naked, suckled with sparks, were chill
Though cotted in a grille of sizzling air
Striped like a convict – black, yellow and red;
Thus were we weaned to knowledge of the Will
That wills the natural world but wills us dead.

O delicate walker, babbler, dialectician Fire,
O enemy and image of ourselves,
Did we not on those mornings after the All Clear,
When you were looting shops in elemental joy
And singing as you swarmed up city block and spire,
Echo your thought in ours? 'Destroy! Destroy!'

Neutrality

The neutral island facing the Atlantic,
The neutral island in the heart of man,
Are bitterly soft reminders of the beginnings
That ended before the end began.

Look into your heart, you will find a County Sligo,
A Knocknarea with for navel a cairn of stones,
You will find the shadow and sheen of a moleskin mountain
And a litter of chronicles and bones.

Look into your heart, you will find fermenting rivers,
Intricacies of gloom and glint,
You will find such ducats of dream and great doubloons of
    ceremony
As nobody to-day would mint.

But then look eastward from your heart, there bulks
A continent, close, dark, as archetypal sin,
While to the west off your own shores the mackerel
Are fat – on the flesh of your kin.

The Springboard

He never made the dive – not while I watched.
High above London, naked in the night
Perched on a board. I peered up through the bars
Made by his fear and mine but it was more than fright
That kept him crucified among the budding stars.

Yes, it was unbelief. He knew only too well
That circumstances called for sacrifice
But, shivering there, spreadeagled above the town,

His blood began to haggle over the price
History would pay if he were to throw himself down.

If it would mend the world, that would be worth while
But he, quite rightly, long had ceased to believe
In any Utopia or in Peace-upon-Earth;
His friends would find in his death neither ransom nor
    reprieve
But only a grain of faith – for what it was worth.

And yet we know he knows what he must do.
There above London where the gargoyles grin
He will dive like a bomber past the broken steeple,
One man wiping out his own original sin
And, like ten million others, dying for the people.

Hiatus

The years that did not count – Civilians in the towns
Remained at the same age as in Nineteen-Thirty-Nine,
Saying last year, meaning the last of peace;
Yet eyes began to pucker, mouth to crease,
The hiatus was too packed with fears and frowns,
The would-be absent heart came forth a magnetic mine.

As if the weekly food queue were to stretch,
Absorb all future Europe. Or as if
The sleepers in the Tube had come from Goya's Spain
Or Thucydides' Corcyra – a long way to fetch
People to prove that civilisation is vain,
Wrapped in old quilts; no wonder they wake stiff.

Yes, we wake stiff and older; especially when
The schoolboys of the Thirties reappear,

Fledged in the void, indubitably men,
Having kept vigil on the Unholy Mount
And found some dark and tentative things made clear,
Some clear made dark, in the years that did not count.

The Streets of Laredo

O early one morning I walked out like Agag,
Early one morning to walk through the fire
Dodging the pythons that leaked on the pavements
With tinkle of glasses and tangle of wire;

When grimed to the eyebrows I met an old fireman
Who looked at me wryly and thus did he say:
'The streets of Laredo are closed to all traffic,
We won't never master this joker to-day.

'O hold the branch tightly and wield the axe brightly,
The bank is in powder, the banker's in hell,
But loot is still free on the streets of Laredo
And when we drive home we drive home on the bell.'

Then out from a doorway there sidled a cockney,
A rocking-chair rocking on top of his head:
'O fifty-five years I been feathering my love-nest
And look at it now – why, you'd sooner be dead.'

At which there arose from a wound in the asphalt,
His big wig a-smoulder, Sir Christopher Wren
Saying: 'Let them make hay of the streets of Laredo;
When your ground-rents expire I will build them again.'

Then twangling their bibles with wrath in their nostrils
From Bonehill Fields came Bunyan and Blake:

'Laredo the golden is fallen, is fallen;
Your flame shall not quench nor your thirst shall not slake.'

'I come to Laredo to find me asylum',
Says Tom Dick and Harry the Wandering Jew;
'They tell me report at the first police station
But the station is pancaked – so what can I do?'

Thus eavesdropping sadly I strolled through Laredo
Perplexed by the dicta misfortunes inspire
Till one low last whisper inveigled my earhole –
The voice of the Angel, the voice of the fire:

O late, very late, have I come to Laredo
A whimsical bride in my new scarlet dress
But at last I took pity on those who were waiting
To see my regalia and feel my caress.

Now ring the bells gaily and play the hose daily,
Put splints on your legs, put a gag on your breath;
O you streets of Laredo, you streets of Laredo,
Lay down the red carpet – My dowry is death.

DEREK MAHON

from Autobiographies
  for Maurice Leitch

I THE HOME FRONT

While the frozen armies trembled
At the gates of Leningrad
They took me home in a taxi
And laid me in my cot,
And there I slept again
With siren and black-out;

And slept under the stairs
Beside the light meter
When bombs fell on the city;
So I never saw the sky
Ablaze with a fiery glow,
Searchlights roaming the stars.

But I do remember one time
(I must have been four then)
Being held up to the window
For a victory parade –
Soldiers, sailors and airmen
Lining the Antrim Road;

And, later, hide-and-seek
Among the air-raid shelters,
The last ration coupons,
Oranges and bananas,
Forage caps and badges
And packets of Lucky Strike.

Gracie Fields on the radio!
Americans in the art-deco
Milk bars! The released Jews
Blinking in shocked sunlight . . .
A male child in a garden
Clutching the *Empire News*.

JOHN MANIFOLD

The Tomb of Lt John Learmonth, AIF

*'At the end on Crete he took to the hills, and said he'd fight it
out with only a revolver. He was a great soldier . . .'*

One of his men in a letter

This is not sorrow, this is work: I build
A cairn of words over a silent man,
My friend John Learmonth whom the Germans killed.

There was no word of hero in his plan;
Verse should have been his love and peace his trade,
But history turned him to a partisan.

Far from the battle as his bones are laid
Crete will remember him. Remember well,
Mountains of Crete, the Second Field Brigade!

Say Crete, and there is little more to tell
Of muddle tall as treachery, despair
And black defeat resounding like a bell;

But bring the magnifying focus near
And in contempt of muddle and defeat
The old heroic virtues still appear.

Australian blood where hot and icy meet
(James Hogg and Lermontov were of his kin)
Lie still and fertilise the fields of Crete.

*

Schoolboy, I watched his ballading begin:
Billy and bullocky and billabong,
Our properties of childhood, all were in.

I heard the air though not the undersong,
the fierceness and resolve; but all the same
They're the tradition, and tradition's strong.

Swagman and bushranger die hard, die game,
Die fighting, like that wild colonial boy –
Jack Dowling, says the ballad, was his name.

He also spun his pistol like a toy,
Turned to the hills like wolf or kangaroo,
And faced destruction with a bitter joy.

His freedom gave him nothing else to do
But set his back against his family tree
And fight the better for the fact he knew

He was as good as dead. Because the sea
Was closed and the air dark and the land lost,
'They'll never capture me alive,' said he.

                    *

That's courage chemically pure, uncrossed
With sacrifice or duty or career,
Which counts and pays in ready coin the cost

Of holding course. Armies are not its sphere
Where all's contrived to achieve its counterfeit;
It swears with discipline, it's volunteer.

I could as hardly make a moral fit
Around it as around a lighting flash.
There is no moral, that's the point of it,

No moral. But I'm glad of this panache
That sparkles, as from flint, from us and steel,
True to no crown nor presidential sash

Nor flag nor fame. Let others mourn and feel
He died for nothing: nothings have their place.
While thus the kind and civilised conceal

This spring of unsuspected inward grace
And look on death as equals, I am filled
With queer affection for the human race.

DAVID MARTIN

Dreams in German

Undated dreams: the sea at Heringsdorf,
The Brocken behind Schierke and the snow
That falls like sugar on the Christmas trees
They're selling in the square. It's hard to know
This land in English. What is Grunewald,
And what is Weissensee and what the name
I seek for her who lies there? All my keys
Are lost. Die Schlüssel sind verloren. Do I still,
As I return to Brandenburg at night,
Declare my landmarks in the tongue I knew,
Say Deutscher Wald when I'm with Rosenrot
Deep in the forest? No, for life went ill
With all my fairies, and in nightmares only
I call by name the giant Schlagetot
Who killed my people and stays close to me
Wherever I may sleep. Yes, not until
He dies shall I go home to childhood. Say it now;
Say Rosenrot, Schneeweisschen, how they came
Tief aus dem Walde, and how Schlagetot
Schlug alle tot and took my book away . . .
Snow White and Rose Red, they are not the same.
Stretch out your hand and gather what is left:
The frieze upon the nursery wall, a light
Kept covered on the landing, or the face
Of Lotte in Charlottenburg that day;
But in translation, like a gazetteer.
Du liebes Land! To call my country dear
Still burns the mouth. But Buchenwald flows right
From German lips into my English ear.

LOYS MASSON

Paris in Tears

Paris in tears Paris soaked Paris as St Veronica
Paris where the Face wipes itself on the pavements as bloody
    as it is
Paris where the Star is the cry of the scalded sweet stoical
    Paris
Widowed mother Paris counting her dead by candle light
Paris of curfews Paris of bonds Paris of pillories
Paris whose voice is a splash of blood on a gag
Paris of bare feet Paris without cartridges Paris O Paris
Where they say Liberty is fighting house by house.

Translated from the French by Hugh Haughton

CZESLAW MIŁOSZ

A Book in the Ruins

A dark building. Crossed boards, nailed up, create
A barrier at the entrance, or a gate
When you go in. Here, in the gutted foyer,
The ivy snaking down the walls is wire
Dangling. And over there the twisted metal
Columns rising from the undergrowth of rubble
Are tattered tree trunks. This could be the brick
Of the library, you don't know yet, or the sick
Grove of dry white aspen where, stalking birds,
You met a Lithuanian dusk stirred
From its silence only by the wails of hawks.
Now walk carefully. You see whole blocks
Of ceiling caved in by a recent blast.
And above, through jagged tiers of plaster,
A patch of blue. Pages of books lying
Scattered at your feet are like fern-leaves hiding
A moldy skeleton, or else fossils
Whitened by the secrets of Jurassic shells.
A remnant life so ancient and unknown
Compels a scientist, tilting a stone
Into the light, to wonder. He can't know
Whether it is some dead epoch's shadow
Or a living form. He looks again
At chalk spirals eroded by the rain,
The rust of tears. Thus, in a book picked up
From the ruins, you see a world erupt
And glitter with its distant sleepy past,
Green times of creatures tumbled to the vast

Abyss and backward: the brows of women,
An earring fixed with trembling hand, pearl button
On a glove, candelabra in the mirror.
The lanterns have been lit. A first shiver
Passes over the instruments. The quadrille
Begins to curl, subdued by the rustle
Of big trees swaying in the formal park.
She slips outside, her shawl floating in the dark,
And meets him in a bower overgrown
With vines. They sit close on a bench of stone
And watch the lanterns glowing in the jasmine.
Or here, this stanza: you hear a goose pen
Creak, the butterfly of an oil lamp
Flutters slowly over scrolls and parchment,
A crucifix, bronze busts. The lines complain,
In plangent rhythms, that desire is vain.
Here a city rises. In the market square
Signboards clang, a stagecoach rumbles in to scare
A flock of pigeons up. Under the town clock,
In the tavern, a hand pauses in the stock
Gesture of arrest – meanwhile workers walk
Home from the textile mill, townsfolk talk
On the steps – and the hand moves now to evoke
The fire of justice, a world gone up in smoke,
The voice quavering with the revenge of ages.
So the world seems to drift from these pages
Like the mist clearing on a field at dawn.
Only when two times, two forms are drawn
Together and their legibility
Disturbed, do you see that immortality
Is not very different from the present
And is for its sake. You pick a fragment
Of grenade which pierced the body of a song

On Daphnis and Chloe. And you long,
Ruefully, to have a talk with her,
As if it were what life prepared you for.
– How is it, Chloe, that your pretty skirt
Is torn so badly by the winds that hurt
Real people, you who, in eternity, sing
The hours, sun in your hair appearing
And disappearing? How is it that your breasts
Are pierced by shrapnel, and the oak groves burn.
While you, charmed, not caring at all, turn
To run through forests of machinery and concrete
And haunt us with the echoes of your feet?
If there is such an eternity, lush
Though short-lived, that's enough. But how . . . hush!
We were predestined to live when the scene
Grows dim and the outline of a Greek ruin
Blackens the sky. It is noon, and wandering
Through a dark building, you see workers sitting
Down to a fire a narrow ray of sunlight
Kindles on the floor. They have dragged out
Heavy books and made a table of them
And begun to cut their bread. In good time
A tank will clatter past, a streetcar chime.

Warsaw, 1941

Translated from the Polish by the author

Flight

When we were fleeing the burning city
And looked back from the first field path,
I said: 'Let the grass grow over our footprints,

Let the harsh prophets fall silent in the fire,
Let the dead explain to the dead what happened.
We are fated to beget a new and violent tribe
Free from the evil and the happiness that drowsed there.
Let us go' – and the earth was opened for us by a sword of
  flames.

Goszyce, 1944

Translated by the author

Café

Of those at the table in the café
where on winter noons a garden of frost glittered on
  windowpanes
I alone survived.
I could go in there if I wanted to
and drumming my fingers in a chilly void
convoke shadows.

With disbelief I touch the cold marble,
with disbelief I touch my own hand.
It – is, and I – am in ever novel becoming,
while they are locked forever and ever
in their last word, their last glance,
and as remote as Emperor Valentinian
or the chiefs of the Massagetes, about whom I know
  nothing,
though hardly one year has passed, or two or three.

I may still cut trees in the woods of the far north,
I may speak from a platform or shoot a film
using techniques they never heard of.

I may learn the taste of fruits from ocean islands
and be photographed in attire from the second half of the
    century.
But they are forever like busts in frock coats and jabots
in some monstrous encyclopedia.

Sometimes when the evening aurora paints the roofs in a
    poor street
and I contemplate the sky, I see in the white clouds
a table wobbling. The waiter whirls with his tray
and they look at me with a burst of laughter
for I still don't know what it is to die at the hand of man,
they know – they know it well.

Warsaw, 1944

Translated by the author

A Poor Christian Looks at the Ghetto

Bees build around red liver,
Ants build around black bone.
It has begun: the tearing, the trampling on silks,
It has begun: the breaking of glass, wood, copper, nickel,
    silver, foam
Of gypsum, iron sheets, violin strings, trumpets, leaves, balls,
    crystals.
Poof! Phosphorescent fire from yellow walls
Engulfs animal and human hair.

Bees build around the honeycomb of lungs,
Ants build around white bone.
Torn is paper, rubber, linen, leather, flax,
Fiber, fabrics, cellulose, snakeskin, wire.

The roof and the wall collapse in flame and heat seizes the
    foundations.
Now there is only the earth, sandy, trodden down,
With one leafless tree.

Slowly, boring a tunnel, a guardian mole makes his way,
With a small red lamp fastened to his forehead.
He touches buried bodies, counts them, pushes on,
He distinguishes human ashes by their luminous vapor,
The ashes of each man by a different part of the spectrum.
Bees build around a red trace.
Ants build around the place left by my body.

I am afraid, so afraid of the guardian mole.
He has swollen eyelids, like a Patriarch
Who has sat much in the light of candles
Reading the great book of the species.

What will I tell him, I, a Jew of the New Testament,
Waiting two thousand years for the second coming of Jesus?
My broken body will deliver me to his sight
And he will count me among the helpers of death:
The uncircumcised.

Warsaw, 1943

Translated by the author

In Distrust of Merits

Strengthened to live, strengthened to die for
  medals and positioned victories?
They're fighting, fighting, fighting the blind
  man who thinks he sees –
who cannot see that the enslaver is
enslaved; the hater, harmed. O shining O
     firm star, O tumultuous
       ocean lashed till small things go
    as they will, the mountainous
      wave makes us who look, know

depth. Lost at sea before they fought! O
  star of David, star of Bethlehem,
O black imperial lion
  of the Lord – emblem
of a risen world – be joined at last, be
joined. There is hate's crown beneath which all is
    death; there's love's without which none
      is king; the blessed deeds bless
    the halo. As contagion
      of sickness makes sickness,

contagion of trust can make trust. They're
  fighting in deserts and caves, one by
one, in battalions and squadrons;
  they're fighting that I
may yet recover from the disease, My
Self; some have it lightly; some will die. 'Man's
    wolf to man' and we devour

ourselves. The enemy could not
have made a greater breach in our
defenses. One pilot-
ing a blind man can escape him, but
Job disheartened by false comfort knew
that nothing can be so defeating
as a blind man who
can see. O alive who are dead, who are
proud not to see, O small dust of the earth
that walks so arrogantly,
trust begets power and faith is
an affectionate thing. We
vow, we make this promise

to the fighting – it's a promise – 'We'll
never hate black, white, red, yellow, Jew,
Gentile, Untouchable.' We are
not competent to
make our vows. With set jaw they are fighting,
fighting, fighting – some we love whom we know,
some we love but know not – that
hearts may feel and not be numb.
It cures me; or am I what
I can't believe in? Some

in snow, some on crags, some in quicksands,
little by little, much by much, they
are fighting fighting fighting that where
there was death there may
be life. 'When a man is prey to anger,
he is moved by outside things; when he holds
his ground in patience patience
patience, that is action or
beauty,' the soldier's defense
and hardest armor for

the fight. The world's an orphans' home. Shall
   we never have peace without sorrow?
without pleas of the dying for
   help that won't come? O
quiet form upon the dust, I cannot
look and yet I must. If these great patient
      dyings – all these agonies
         and wound-bearings and bloodshed –
      can teach us how to live, these
         dyings were not wasted.

Hate-hardened heart, O heart of iron,
   iron is iron till it is rust.
There never was a war that was
   not inward; I must
fight till I have conquered in myself what
causes war, but I would not believe it.
      I inwardly did nothing.
         O Iscariot-like crime!
      Beauty is everlasting
         and dust is for a time.

'Keeping Their World Large'
All too literally, their flesh and their spirit are our shield.
New York Times, June 7, 1944

   I should like to see that country's tiles, bedrooms, stone
      patios
      and ancient wells: Rinaldo
Caramonica's the cobbler's, Frank Sblendorio's
      and Dominick Angelastro's country –
      the grocer's, the iceman's, the dancer's – the
beautiful Miss Damiano's; wisdom's

and all angels' Italy, this Christmas Day
this Christmas year.
    A noiseless piano, an
innocent war, the heart that can act against itself. Here,
    each unlike and all alike, could
    so many – stumbling, falling, multiplied
till bodies lay as ground to walk on –

    'If Christ and the apostles died in vain,
I'll die in vain with them'
    against this way of victory.
That forest of white crosses!
    My eyes won't close to it.
    All laid like animals for sacrifice –
like Isaac on the mount, were their own sacrifice.

    Marching to death, marching to life?
'Keeping their world large,'
    whose spirits and whose bodies
all too literally were our shield,
    are still our shield.
    They fought the enemy,
we fight fat living and self-pity.
    Shine, o shine,
unfalsifying sun, on this sick scene.

Hitler Spring

And she to see whom all the heavens turn
  Dante (?) to Giovanni Querini

Thickly the whitened cloud from the maddened moths
whirls round the pallid standards and on the embankments,
spreads on the ground a pall that crackles
like sugar underfoot: now imminent summer releases
the night frost that it knew
in the dead seasons' secret quarries
in the gardens that from Maiano come leaping down to
  these sandbeds.

Down the corso just now there passed a herald of hell
in flight through the cheering assassins, and a mystic gulf of
  fire
beflagged with crooked crosses took him and swallowed
  him,
the poor shops have been shuttered
inoffensive though they too were armed
with cannons and toys of war,
the butcher has put up his bars, the one who adorned
the snouts of goat kids he had slain with berries,
the solemnities of still bloodless myths of killers
have turned into a filthy morris-feast of flattened wings
of ghosts on the mudflats, and the water goes on gnawing
the banks and no man is any longer blameless.

Was all for nought then? – the Roman candles
that slowly whitened the horizon at San Giovanni
and the pledges and the long good byes

strong as a baptism in mournful expectation
of the horde (but a jewel shot the air distilling
on the ice and shorelands of your coasts
Tobits angels, the seven, the seed
of the future) and the heliotropes born
of your hands – burnt and sucked dry
by the pollen that crackles like fire
and stabs like a sleety wind . . .
   Oh the wounded
spring is still festive if this death
freezes again in death. Once anew
look upward Clizia, it is your fate, you
who in all change preserve your love unchanged
until the blinded sun you bear within you
is dazzled in the Other or is confounded
with Him, for all. Perhaps the alarms and sirens
welcoming these monsters in the evening
of their witches sabbath are already mingling
with the sound unleashed from heaven, descending,
   conquering –
with a breath of dawn that may be manifest
for all, to-morrow, white but without wings
of horror in the burnt gravel of the south . . .

Translated from the Italian by Bernard Wall

WILLIAM MONTGOMERIE

The Edge of the War

On the esplanade
the deck-chair hirer
watches his summer
shovelled into sandbags
till at high tide
the beach is flooded to the Promenade

Our submarines like five alligators
pass
always at dusk
to the North Sea
where a German plane has sown surface mines

One mine circles the harbour slowly
missing the pier
again and again and again
until defused by a simple twist of the wrist

The whelk-seller leaves his bag and barrow
to pull a mine up the beach
and dies
'Stretchers! Stretchers here!'
they shout from the Castle

A policeman arrests one mine on the shore
and drags it halfway to the police-station
his tombstone a cottage gable-end
pocked with holes packed with red putty

[186]

Casks of brandy butter and ham
float on to the beach
from a mined ship

A grocer's van parks at dusk
by the Castle railings
Sergeant MacPherson pins on his notice board
'Flotsam butter from the beach
must be left immediately
at the police-station'

For days the streets are sweet
with the smell of shortbread

Blue-mould butter
is dumped on the counter
or thrown at night
over the wall of the station
where greased door-handles will not turn

A German plane
following the wrong railway
dumps his bombs on an up-country farm

A plane from the North-Sea sunrise
machine-gunning our little fishing fleet
brushes a wing against a mast
and ditches

'*Hilfe! Hilfe!*'

'Take your time lads!'
shouts a skipper
to a drifter turning toward the sinking plane

'One of our planes
has sunk a German U-boat
off Montrose'

A war-rumour

The submarine
one of ours
dented
is in dry-dock
in Dundee

Bennet from Stratford-on-Avon
one of the crew
cycles to our house
with no lights
sings to us
of Boughton's Lordly Ones
from *The Immortal Hour*
talks of his wife in Stratford
and of the night they watched Birmingham burning

After late supper
he returns to the night
having left his ration of pipe-tobacco
on the piano

If his submarine sinks
he knows how to escape
and is found afloat
on the Pacific Ocean
drowned

On Tents Muir
across the Tay estuary

parachutes are falling
from war planes

We talk of the Second Front

One parachute does not open

Broughty Ferry

VLADIMIR NABOKOV

'No matter how the Soviet tinsel glitters'

No matter how the Soviet tinsel glitters
Upon the canvas of a battle piece;
No matter how the soul dissolves in pity,
I will not bend, I will not cease

Loathing the filth, brutality and boredom
Of silent servitude. No, no, I shout,
My spirit is still quick, still exile-hungry,
I'm still a poet, count me out!

1944, Cambridge, Mass.

Translated from the Russian by the author

ÁGNES NEMES NAGY

Lazarus

He sat up slowly, and around his left side
all his long life's muscles ached.
His death was torn from him like caked
gauze. Rising was as hard as having died.

Translated from the Hungarian by Frederic Will

To a Poet

My contemporary. He died, not I.
He fell near Tobruk, poor boy.
He was English. Other names, for us,
tell the places where, like ripe nuts,
heads fell and cracked in twos,
those portable radios,
their poise of parts and volume
finer than the Eiffel, lovely spinal column
as it crashed down to the earth.
That's how I think of your youth –
like a dotard who doesn't know
now from fifty years ago,
his heart in twilight, addlepated.

But love is complicated.

Translated by Bruce Berlind

A Fable of the War

The full moon is partly hidden by cloud,
The snow that fell when we came off the boat
Has stopped by now, and it is turning colder.
I pace the platform under the blue lights,
Under a frame of glass and emptiness
In a station whose name I do not know.

Suddenly, passing the known and unknown
Bowed faces of my company, the sad
And potent outfit of the armed, I see
That we are dead. By stormless Acheron
We stand easy, and the occasional moon
Strikes terribly from steel and bone alike.

Our flesh, I see, was too corruptible
For the huge work of death. Only the blind
Crater of the eye can suffer well
The midnight cold of stations in no place,
And hold the tears of pity frozen that
They will implacably reflect on war.

But I have read that God let Solomon
Stand upright, although dead, until the temple
Should be raised up, that demons forced to the work
Might not revolt before the thing was done.
And the king stood, until a little worm
Had eaten through the stick he leaned upon.

So gentlemen – by greatcoat, cartridge belt
And helmet held together for the time –

In honourably enduring her we seek
The second death. Until the worm shall bite
To betray us, lean each man upon his gun
That the great work not falter but go on.

Redeployment

They say the war is over. But water still
Comes bloody from the taps, and my pet cat
In his disorder vomits worms which crawl
Swiftly away. Maybe they leave the house.
These worms are white, and flecked with the cat's blood.

The war may be over. I know a man
Who keeps a pleasant souvenir, he keeps
A soldier's dead blue eyeballs that he found
Somewhere – hard as chalk, and blue as slate.
He clicks them in his pocket while he talks.

And now there are cockroaches in the house,
They get slightly drunk on DDT,
Are fast, hard, shifty – can be drowned but not
Without you hold them under quite some time.
People say the Mexican kind can fly.

The end of the war. I took it quietly
Enough. I tried to wash the dirt out of
My hair and from under my fingernails,
I dressed in clean white clothes and went to bed.
I heard the dust falling between the walls.

LORINE NIEDECKER

Wartime

I left my baby in Forest A
quivering toward light:
Keep warm, dear thing, drink from the cow –
her stillness is alive

You in the leaves sweetly growing –
survive these plants upheaved
with noise and flame, learn change
in strategy.

I think of Joe who never knew
where his baby went
and Mary heavy, peace or war,
no child, no enlightenment.

Bombings

You could go to the Underground's platform
for a three half-penny tube fare;
safe vaults of the Bank of England
you couldn't go there.

The sheltered slept
under eiderdown,
Lady Diana and the Lord himself
in apartments deep in the ground.

GEORGE OPPEN

from Of Being Numerous: 14

I cannot even now
Altogether disengage myself
From those men

With whom I stood in emplacements, in mess tents,
In hospitals and sheds and hid in the gullies
Of blasted roads in a ruined country,

Among them many men
More capable than I –

Muykut and a sergeant
Named Healy,
That lieutenant also –

How forget that? How talk
Distantly of 'The People'

Who are that force
Within the walls
Of cities

Wherein their cars

Echo like history
Down walled avenues
In which one cannot speak.

Myth of the Blaze

night   sky   bird's   world
to know   to know   in my life to know

what I have said to myself

the dark to escape in brilliant highways
of the night sky, finally
why had they not

killed me why did they fire that warning
wounding cannon only the one round I hold a
    superstition

because of this   lost to be lost   Wyatt's
lyric and Rezi's
running thru my mind
in the destroyed (and guilty) Theatre
of the War   I'd cried
and remembered
boyhood   degradation   other
degradations and this crime I will not recover
from that landscape it will be in my mind
it will fill my mind and this is horrible
death bed   pavement   the secret taste
of being lost

dead

clown in the birds'
world what names
(but my name)

and my love's name to speak

into the eyes
of the Tyger   blaze

of changes . . . 'named

the animals'   name

and name the vigorous dusty strong

animals gather
under the joists   the boards   older

than they   giving
them darkness the gifted

dark tho names   the names   the 'little'

adventurous
words   a mountain   the cliff

a wave are taxonomy I believe

in the world

because it is
impossible   the shack

on the coast

under the eaves
the rain barrel flooding

in the weather and no lights

across rough water illumined
as tho the narrow

end of the funnel what are the names
of the Tyger   to speak
to the eyes

of the Tiger   blaze
of the tiger   who moves in the forest leaving

no scent

but the pine needles' his eyes blink

quick
in   the shack
in the knife-cut
and the opaque

white

bread each side of the knife

DAN PAGIS

Written in Pencil in the Sealed Railway-Car

here in this carload
i am eve
with abel my son
if you see my other son
cain son of man
tell him that i

Translated from the Hebrew by Stephen Mitchell

The Roll Call

He stands, stamps a little in his boots,
rubs his hands. He's cold in the morning breeze:
a diligent angel, who worked hard for his promotions.
Suddenly he thinks he's made a mistake: all eyes,
he counts again in the open notebook
all the bodies waiting for him in the square,
camp within camp: only I
am not there, am not there, am a mistake,
turn off my eyes, quickly, erase my shadow.
I shall not want. The sum will be all right
without me: here forever.

Translated by Stephen Mitchell

Testimony

No no: they definitely were
human beings: uniforms, boots.
How to explain? They were created
in the image.

I was a shade.
A different creator made me.

And he in his mercy left nothing of me that would die.
And I fled to him, floated up weightless, blue,
forgiving – I would even say: apologising –
smoke to omnipotent smoke
that has no face or image.

Translated by Stephen Mitchell

Instructions for Crossing the Border

Imaginary man, go. Here is your passport.
You are not allowed to remember.
You have to match the description:
your eyes are already blue.
Don't escape with the sparks
inside the smokestack:
you are a man, you sit in the train.
Sit comfortably.
You've got a decent coat now,
a repaired body, a new name
ready in your throat.
Go. You are not allowed to forget.

Translated by Stephen Mitchell

Draft of a Reparations Agreement

All right, gentlemen who cry blue murder as always,
nagging miracle-makers,
quiet!
Everything will be returned to its place,
paragraph after paragraph.
The scream back into the throat.
The gold teeth back to the gums.
The terror.
The smoke back to the tin chimney and further on and
    inside
back to the hollow of the bones,
and already you will be covered with skin and sinews and
    you will live,
look, you will have your lives back,
sit in the living room, read the evening paper.
Here you are. Nothing is too late.
As to the yellow star:
it will be torn from your chest
immediately
and will emigrate
to the sky.

Translated by Stephen Mitchell

The Old Park

A small boy in a little bed.
Savagely roars the storm.
Nines of cawing rooks fly off,
Scatter and re-form.

A doctor in a white coat
Was swabbing a stitched limb,
When the patient recognised
A childhood friend, his fathers' home.

Again he's in the old park.
Frosty mornings flash again,
And when they put on compresses,
Tears run down the outer pane.

Voices of this century
And visions of the last
Interweave as nurses' hands
Make his bandage fast.

People walk across the ward,
Doors bang in the corridor.
Gun batteries thud dully
Beyond the lake's far shore.

Lower sinks the setting sun.
It pierced the creek, withdrew,
And levelling its lance,
It runs the distance through.

And two minutes later, outside,
Into the craters flow
Wave on wave of emerald
As in a magic lantern show.

Pain attacks more fiercely,
Stronger the wind, fiercer the storm,
And nines of rooks, black nines of clubs
Scatter and re-form.

Turbulence contorts the limes,
Wind bends them to the ground,
And hearing the branches groan,
The patient forgets his wound.

Legends have aged the park.
Napoleon camped here,
And Samarin the Slavophil
Served and was buried near.

Descendant of the Decembrist,
Great-grandson of a heroine,
Here he shot at cawing crows
And overcame Latin.

If only he has strength enough,
The new enthusiast will
Revise his great-grandfather's works,
Edit the Slavophil.

He himself will write a play
Inspired by the war,
Thinks the patient lying there,
Hearing the forest roar.

The unimaginable course
Of life undreamt-of then
Will be plotted and revealed
By a provincial pen.

1943

Translated from the Russian by Jon Stallworthy and Peter France

Fresco Come to Life

Again the shells were falling.
As on board ship, the cloud
And night sky over Stalingrad
Rocked in a plaster shroud.

Earth droned, as if in prayer
To ward off the shrieking shell,
And with its censer threw up smoke
And rubble where it fell.

Whenever, between fighting, he
Went round his company under fire,
A sense of strange familiarity
Haunted him like desire.

These hedgehog buildings, where could he
Have seen their bottomless holes before?
The evidence of past bombardments
Seemed fabulous and familiar.

What did it mean, the four-armed sign,
Enclosed in the pitch-black frame?
Of whom did they remind him,
The smashed floors and the flame?

And suddenly he saw his childhood,
His childhood, and the monastery; heard
The penitents, and in the garden
The nightingale and mocking-bird.

He gripped his mother with a son's hand,
And devils, fearing the archangel's spear,
Leaped from the chapel's sombre frescos
Into just such pits as here.

And the boy saw himself in armour.
Defending his mother in shining mail,
And fell upon the evil one
With its swastika-tipped tail.

And nearby in a mounted duel
Saint George shone down on the dragon,
And water-lilies studded the pond
And birds sang crazily on and on.

The fatherland, like the forest's voice,
A call in the wood and the wood's echo,
Beckoned with an alluring music
And smelt of budding birch and willow.

How he remembers those clearings
Now, when in pursuit he impales
And tramples enemy tanks
For all their fearful dragon scales.

He has crossed the frontiers of the world,
And the future, like the firmament,
Already rages, not a dream,
Approaching, and magnificent.

1944

Translated by Jon Stallworthy and Peter France

JÁNOS PILINSKY

Frankfurt 1945

In the river bank, an empty sandpit –
all that summer we took the refuse there.
Gliding among villas and gardens
we came to a bridge. Then a dip of the road
and the wooden fence of the racetrack.
A few jolts, and the truck began to slow down.
But even before the brakes could tighten
the first surge of hunger overwhelmed us.

Among the spilling buckets and the bursting sacks –
horror of the spines, stooping into position!
Then among those toppled crates began
the pitiless pre-censorship,
interrogating the gristles of the offal.
And there, on all fours, hunger
could not stomach its own fury,
but revolted and surrendered.

They were lost in the dust and filth.
The whole truck shook, howling.
The swill clogged their hearts
and swamped their consciousness.
They burrowed to the bottoms of the filled cans
till their mouths and eyes were caked.
They drowned in that living sludge
and there they were resurrected with heads buried.

And they brought back, scrap by scrap,
what had been utterly lost with them,

wringing their salvation, drunkenly,
out of the gouged mush –
but before their joy could properly be seized
the poison of comprehension stirred.
First, only the bitterness in their mouths,
then their hearts tasted the full sadness.

Abruptly, they backed from the mob. Almost sober
they watched how this intoxication –
betraying their misery –
possessed their whole being.
But then again they abandoned themselves utterly,
now only enduring till their organs
cramming themselves, should have completed
the last mistake of gratification.

Only to get away – no matter where!
Only to get out, now!
The glowing pack drove us from them
without a flash! They did not even touch us.
All around – the blank walls of the pit.
Only to get home! Probably a steamer
went past quite close by on the river below
and its smoke and soot screened perfectly

the steep, crooked exit. Out across the field!
Bounding eagerly over the mounds
on to the flaming concrete. Then the villas!
The green world streaming back!
The wooden fence of the racecourse.
And after the volley of gaps between the palings
the torrid air, swooning from the gardens!
Then all at once – the shock of loneliness!

In a moment the splendour of the foliage burned out –
its flame hung darkly to the road.
And our faces, and our hands, darkened.
And with us, the paradise.
While behind us, between the jouncing cans
and the tattered dusty trees
emerged the crepuscular city
of Frankfurt – 1945.

> *Translated from the Hungarian by Ted Hughes*
> *and János Csokits*

The French Prisoner

If only I could forget that Frenchman.
I saw him, a little before dawn, creeping past our hut
into the dense growth of the back garden
so that he almost merged into the ground.
As I watched he looked back, he peered all round –
at last he had found a safe hideout.
Now his plunder can be all his!
Whatever happens, he'll go no further.

And already he is eating, biting into the turnip
which he must have smuggled out under his rags.
He was gulping raw cattle-turnip!
Yet he had hardly swallowed one mouthful
before it vomited back up.
Then the sweet pulp in his mouth mingled
with joy and revulsion the same
as the happy and unhappy are coupled
in their bodies' ravenous ecstasy.

Only to forget that body, those convulsed shoulder blades,
the hands shrunk to bone,
the bare palm that crammed at his mouth, and clung there
so that it ate, too.
And the shame, desperate, furious,
of the organs savaging each other,
forced to tear from each other
their last shreds of kinship.

The way his clumsy feet had been left out
of the gibbering, bestial elation –
and splayed there, squashed beneath
the torture and rapture of his body.
And his glance – if only I could forget that!
Though he was choking, he kept on
forcing more down his gullet – no matter what –
only to eat – anything – this – that – even himself!

Why go on. Guards came for him.
He had escaped from the nearby prison camp.
And just as I did then, in that garden,
I am strolling here, among garden shadows, at home.
I look into my notes and quote:
'If only I could forget that Frenchman . . .'
And from my ears, from my eyes, my mouth
the scorching memory roars at me:

'I am hungry!' And suddenly I feel
the everlasting hunger
that poor creature has long since forgotten
and which no earthly nourishment can lessen.
He lives on me. And more and more hungrily!
And I am less and less sufficient for him.

And now he, who would have eaten anything,
is yelling for my heart.

Translated by Ted Hughes and János Csokits

On the Wall of a KZ-Lager

Where you have fallen, you stay.
In the whole universe, this is your place.
Just this single spot.
But you have made this yours utterly.

The countryside evades you.
House, mill, poplar,
each thing strives to be free of you
as if it were mutating in nothingness.

But now it is you who stay.
Did we blind you? You continue to watch us.
Did we rob you? You enriched yourself.
Speechless, speechless, you testify against us.

Translated by Ted Hughes and János Csokits

FRANCIS PONGE

Metamorphosis

You can twist the elastic of your heart
Round the foot of the stalks
But it's not as a caterpillar
You will know the flowers
When more than one sign announces
Your rush towards happiness

He trembles and with a single leap
Rejoins the butterflies.

Translated from the French by Hugh Haughton

EZRA POUND

from Canto LXXIV

The enormous tragedy of the dream in the peasant's bent
  shoulders
  Manes! Manes was tanned and stuffed,
  Thus Ben and la Clara *a Milano*
        by the heels at Milano
That maggots shd/ eat the dead bullock
DIGONOS, Δίγονος, but the twice crucified
        where in history will you find it?
yet say this to the Possum: a bang, not a whimper,
  with a bang not with a whimper,
To build the city of Dioce whose terraces are the colour of
  stars.
The suave eyes, quiet, not scornful,
        rain also is of the process.
What you depart from is not the way
and olive tree blown white in the wind
washed in the Kiang and Han
what whiteness will you add to this whiteness,
        what candor?
'the great periplum brings in the stars to our shore.'
You who have passed the pillars and outward from Herakles
when Lucifer fell in N. Carolina.
if the suave air give way to scirocco
ΟΫ ΤΙΣ, ΟΫ ΤΙΣ? Odysseus
        the name of my family.
the wind also is of the process,
        sorella la luna
Fear god and the stupidity of the populace,

but a precise definition
   transmitted thus Sigismundo
   thus Duccio, thus Zuan Bellin, or trastevere with La Sposa
Sponsa Cristi in mosaic till our time / deification of emperors
but a snotty barbarian ignorant of T'ang history need not
   deceive one
nor Charlie Sung's money on loan from anonimo
that is, we suppose Charlie had some
and in India the rate down to 18 per hundred
but the local loan lice provided from imported bankers
so the total interest sweated out of the Indian farmers
     rose in Churchillian grandeur
as when, and plus when, he returned to the putrid gold
   standard
as was about 1925   Oh my England
that free speech without free radio speech is as zero
     and but one point needed for Stalin
you need not, i.e. need not take over the means of
   production;
money to signify work done, inside a system
    and measured and wanted
'I have not done unnecessary manual labour'
says the R.C. chaplain's field book
        (preparation before confession)
squawky as larks over the death cells
       militarism progressing westward
im Westen nichts neues
and the Constitution in jeopardy
and that state of things not very new either

'of sapphire, for this stone giveth sleep'
not words whereto to be faithful
   nor deeds that they be resolute

only that bird-hearted equity make timber
          and lay hold of the earth
and Rouse found they spoke of Elias
in telling the tales of Odysseus   OὟ ΤΙΣ
                              OὟ ΤΙΣ
'I am noman, my name is noman'
but Wanjina is, shall we say, Ouan Jin
or the man with an education
and whose mouth was removed by his father
          because he made too many *things*
whereby cluttered the bushman's baggage
vide the expedition of Frobenius' pupils about 1938
                              to Auss 'ralia
Ouan Jin spoke and thereby created the named
                              thereby making clutter
the bane of men moving
and so his mouth was removed
as you will find it removed in his pictures
          in principio verbum
          paraclete or the verbum perfectum: sinceritas
from the death cells in sight of Mt. Taishan @ Pisa
as Fujiyama at Gardone
when the cat walked the top bar of the railing
and the water was still on the West side
flowing toward the Villa Catullo
where with sound ever moving
               in diminutive poluphloisboios
in the stillness outlasting all wars

JACQUES PRÉVERT

Barbara

Remember Barbara
It rained all day on Brest that day
And you walked smiling
Flushed enraptured streaming-wet
In the rain
Remember Barbara
It rained all day on Brest that day
And I ran into you in Siam Street
You were smiling
And I smiled too
Remember Barbara
You whom I didn't know
You who didn't know me
Remember
Remember that day still
Don't forget
A man was taking cover on a porch
And he cried your name
Barbara
And you ran to him in the rain
Streaming-wet enraptured flushed
And you threw yourself in his arms
Remember that Barbara
And don't be mad if I speak familiarly
I speak familiarly to everyone I love
Even if I've seen them only once
I speak familiarly to all who are in love
Even if I don't know them

Remember Barbara
Don't forget
That good and happy rain
On your happy face
On that happy town
That rain upon the sea
Upon the arsenal
Upon the Ushant boat
Oh Barbara
What shitstupidity the war
Now what's become of you
Under this iron rain
Of fire and steel and blood
And he who held you in his arms
Amorously
Is he dead and gone or still so much alive
Oh Barbara
It's rained all day on Brest today
As it was raining before
But it isn't the same anymore
And everything is wrecked
It's a rain of mourning terrible and desolate
Nor is it still a storm
Of iron and steel and blood
But simply clouds
That die like dogs
Dogs that disappear
In the downpour drowning Brest
And float away to rot
A long way off
A long long way from Brest
Of which there's nothing left.

Translated from the French by Lawrence Ferlinghetti

F. T. PRINCE

Soldiers Bathing

The sea at evening moves across the sand.
Under a reddening sky I watch the freedom of a band
Of soldiers who belong to me. Stripped bare
For bathing in the sea, they shout and run in the warm air;
Their flesh, worn by the trade of war, revives
And my mind towards the meaning of it strives.

All's pathos now. The body that was gross,
Rank, ravenous, disgusting in the act or in repose,
All fever, filth and sweat, its bestial strength
And bestial decay, by pain and labour grows at length
Fragile and luminous. 'Poor bare forked animal'
Conscious of his desires and needs and flesh that rise and
    fall,
Stands in the soft air, tasting after toil
The sweetness of his nakedness; letting the sea-waves coil
Their frothy tongues about his feet, forgets
His hatred of the war, its terrible pressure that begets
A machinery of death and slavery,
Each being a slave and making slaves of others; finds that he
Remembers lovely freedom in a game,
Mocking himself, and comically mimics fear and shame.

He plays with death and animality,
And reading in the shadows of his pallid flesh, I see
The idea of Michelangelo's cartoon
Of soldiers bathing, breaking off before they were half done
At some sortie of the enemy, an episode
On the Pisan wars with Florence. I remember now he
    showed

Their muscular limbs that clamber from the water,
And heads that turn across the shoulder, eager for the
    slaughter,
Forgetful of their bodies that are bare,
And hot to buckle on and use the weapons lying there.
And I think too of the theme another found
When, shadowing men's bodies on a sinister red ground,
Another Florentine, Pollaiuolo,
Painted a naked battle; warriors, straddled, hacked the foe,
Dug their bare toes into the ground and slew
The brother – naked man who lay between their feet and
    drew
His lips back from his teeth in a grimace,
And showed the thing suspended, stripped; a theme
Born out of the experience of war's horrible extreme
Beneath a sky where even the air flows
With 'lacrimae Christi'. For that rage, that bitterness, those
    blows
That hatred of the slain, what could it be
But indirectly or directly a commentary
On the Crucifixion? And the picture burns
With indignation and pity and despair by turns,
Because it is the obverse of the scene
Where Christ hangs murdered, stripped, upon the Cross. I
    mean
That is the explanation of its rage.
And we too have our bitterness and pity that engage
Blood, spirit in this war. But night begins,
Night of the mind; who nowadays is conscious of our sins?
Though every human deed concerns our blood,
And even we must know, what nobody has understood,
That some great love is over all we do,
And that is what has driven us to this fury, for so few

Can suffer all the terror of that love.
The terror of that love has set us spinning in this groove
Greased with our blood. These dry themselves and dress,
Combing their hair, forget the fear and shame of nakedness.
Because to love is frightening we prefer
The freedom of our crimes. Yet as I drink the dusky air
I feel a strange delight that fills me full,
Strange gratitude, as if evil itself were beautiful
And kiss the wound in thought, while in the west
I watch a streak of red that might have issued from Christ's
  breast.

Man of My Time

You are still the one with the stone and the sling,
man of my time. You were in the cockpit,
with the malign wings, the sundials of death,
– I have seen you – in the chariot of fire, at the gallows,
at the wheels of torture. I have seen you: it was you,
with your exact science persuaded to extermination,
without love, without Christ. Again, as always, you
have killed, as did your fathers kill, as did
the animals that saw you for the first time, kill.
And this blood smells as on the day
one brother told the other brother: 'Let us
go into the fields.' And that echo, chill, tenacious,
has reached down to you, within your day.
Forget, o sons, the clouds of blood
risen from the earth, forget the fathers:
their tombs sink down in ashes,
black birds, the wind, cover their heart.

Translated from the Italian by Allen Mandelbaum

January 19, 1944

I read to you an ancient one's soft verses,
and the words that were born among the vineyards,
the tents, on the riverbanks of eastern lands,
how sad and desolate they fall in this
profoundest night of war, where no one

crosses the sky of the angels of death,
and the wind is a ruinous roar when it tosses
the metal sheets that here, on high,
divide the balconies, the melancholy
rises from dogs that howl in the gardens
at the rifle shots of the patrols
on the empty streets. Someone's alive.
Perhaps someone's alive. But we, here,
attentive to the ancient voice,
seek a sign that overarches life
the obscure sorcery of earth,
where even among the rubble tombs
the malign grass raises up its flower.

Translated by Allen Mandelbaum

On the Branches of the Willows

And how could we have sung
with the foreign foot on our heart,
among the dead abandoned in the squares
on the grass set hard with ice, at the lamb-like
cry of children, at the black howl
of the mother advancing on her son
crucified on the telegraph pole?
On the branches of the willows, as a vow,
our poets' lyres were hanging,
swinging just a little in the dismal wind.

Translated by Geoff Page and Loredana Nardi-Ford

MIKLÓS RADNÓTI

The Second Eclogue

Pilot:
Last night. We went far. In rage, I laughed, I was so mad.
Their fighters were all droning like a bee-swarm overhead.
Their defence was strong and, friend, oh how they fired and
    fired –
Till over the horizon our relief squadron appeared.
I just missed being shot down and scraped together below,
But see! I am back and, tomorrow, this craven Europe shall
    know
Fear in air-raid shelters, as they tremble hidden away . . .
But enough of that, let's leave it. Have you written since
    yesterday?

Poet:
I have. The poet writes, as dogs howl or cats mew
Or small fish coyly spawn. What else am I to do?
I write about everything – write even for you, up there,
So that flying you may know of my life and of how I fare
When between the rows of houses, blown up and tumbling
    down,
The bloodshot light of the moon reels drunkenly around,
When the city squares bulge, all of them terror-stricken,
Breathing stops, and even the sky will seem to sicken,
And the planes keep coming on, then disappear, and then
Swoop, like jabbering madness, down from the sky again.
I write; what else can I do? If you knew how dangerous
A poem can be, how frail, how capricious a single verse . . .
For that involves courage too – you see? Poets must write,

[222]

Cats mew, dogs howl, small fish . . . and so on; but you who
    fight,
What do you know? Nothing. You listen, but all you hear
Is the plane you have just left, as it drones on in your ear.
No use denying it, friend. It's become a part of you.
What do you think about as you fly above in the blue?

Pilot:
Laugh at me, but I'm scared. And I long to lie in repose
Beside my love on a bed, and for these eyes to close.
Or else, under my breath, I would softly hum her a tune
In the wild and steamy chaos of the flying-men's canteen.
Up there I want to come down, down here to be back in
    space:
In this world moulded for me, for me there is no place.
And I know full well, I have grown too fond of my
    aeroplane –
True, but if hit, the rhythm we suffer at is the same . . .
But you know and will write about it! It won't be a secret
    that I,
Who now just destroy, homeless between the earth and the
    sky,
Lived as a man lives. Alas, who'd understand or believe it?
Will you write of me?

Poet: If I live, if there's anyone left to read it.

27 April 1941

Translated from the Hungarian by Clive Wilmer
and George Gömöri

A La Recherche

You too, past gentle evenings, are being refined into
    memory!
Bright table, once adorned by poets and their young women,
Where in the mud of the past, now, do you slide away to?
Where is the night when friends, sparkling with wit and
    gusto,
Still drank their fine hock gaily from bright-eyed slender
    glasses?

Lines of poetry swam around in the lamplight, brilliant
Green adjectives swayed on the metre's foaming crest and
Those who are dead now were living, the prisoners still
    home, and all of
Those dear friends who are missing, the long-ago-fallen,
    wrote poems.
Their hearts are under the soil of Flanders, Ukraine and
    Iberia.

There were men of a kind who gritted their teeth, ran into
    gunfire
And fought – only because they could do nothing against it,
And while the company – the filthy night their shelter –
Slept restlessly round them, they'd be thinking of rooms
    they'd lived in: –
Islands and caves to them inside this hostile order.

There were places they travelled to in tight-sealed cattle-
    wagons.
They had to stand in minefields: they were unarmed and
    freezing.
There was also a place they went to, guns in their hands and
    willing,

Without a word: they saw their own cause in that struggle.
And now the angel of freedom guards their deep dream
  nightly.

There were places . . . No matter. Where are the wise, wine-
  drinking parties?
Their call-up papers flew to them, fragmentary poems
  multiplied,
And wrinkles multiplied, too, around the lips and under
The eyes of young women with lovely smiles: sylph-like in
  bearing
They grew to be heavy in the silent years of wartime.

Where is the night, the bar, the table under the lime-trees?
And those still alive, where are they – those herded into the
  battle?
My hand still clasps their hands, my heart still hears their
  voices.
I recall their works, I perceive the stature of their torsos
Which appear to me, silent prisoner, on the wailing heights
  of Serbia.

Where is the night? That night will never more come back to
  us,
For whatever has passed on, death alters its perspectives.
They sit down at the table, they hide in the smiles of women,
And will sip wine from our glasses: they who now, unburied,
Sleep in far-away forests, sleep in distant pastures.

Lager Heideman, 17 August 1944

Translated by Clive Wilmer and George Gömöri

Postcards

I

From Bulgaria, wild and swollen, the noise of cannon rolls;
It booms against the ridge, then hesitates, and falls.
Men, animals, carts, thoughts pile up as they fly;
The road rears back and whinnies, maned is the racing sky.
But you, in this shifting chaos, are what in me is constant:
In my soul's depth forever, you shine – you are as silent
And motionless, as an angel who marvels at destruction,
Or a beetle burrowing in a hollow tree's corruption.

In the mountains, 30 August 1944

II

No more than six or seven miles away
Haystacks and houses flare;
There, on the meadows' verges, peasants crouch,
Pipe-smoking, dumb with fear.
Here still, where the tiny shepherdess steps in,
Ripples on the lake spread;
A flock of ruffled sheep bend over it
And drink the clouds they tread.

Cservenka, 6 October 1944

III

Blood-red, the spittle drools from the oxen's mouths,
The men, stooping to urinate, pass blood,
The squad stands bunched in groups whose reek disgusts.
And loathsome death blows overhead in gusts.

Mohács, 24 October 1944

IV

I fell beside him. His body – which was taut
As a cord is, when it snaps – spun as I fell.
Shot in the neck. 'This is how you will end,'
I whispered to myself. 'Keep lying still.
Now, patience is flowering into death.'
'*Der springt noch auf*,' said someone over me.
Blood on my ears was drying, caked with earth.

Szentkirályszabadja, 31 October 1944

Translated by Clive Wilmer and George Gömöri

HERBERT READ

To a Conscript of 1940

Qui n'a pas une fois désespéré de l'honneur,
ne sera jamais un héros.

Georges Bernanos

A soldier passed me in the freshly fallen snow
His footsteps muffled, his face unearthly grey;
And my heart gave a sudden leap
As I gazed on a ghost of five-and-twenty years ago.

I shouted Halt! and my voice had the old accustomed ring
And he obeyed it as it was obeyed
In the shrouded days when I too was one
Of an army of young men marching

Into the unknown. He turned towards me and I said:
'I am one of those who went before you
Five-and-twenty years ago: one of the many who never
    returned,
Of the many who returned and yet were dead.

'We went where you are going, into the rain and the mud;
We fought as you will fight
With death and darkness and despair;
We gave what you will give – our brains and our blood.

'We think we gave in vain. The world was not renewed.
There was hope in the homestead and anger in the streets
But the old world was restored and we returned
To the dreary field and workshop, and the immemorial feud

'Of rich and poor. Our victory was our defeat.
Power was retained where power had been misused

[228]

And youth was left to sweep away
The ashes that the fires had strewn beneath our feet.

'But one thing we learned: there is no glory in the deed
Until the soldier wears a badge of tarnished braid;
There are heroes who have heard the rally and have seen
The glitter of a garland round their head.

'Theirs is the hollow victory. They are deceived.
But you, my brother and my ghost, if you can go
Knowing that there is no reward, no certain use
In all your sacrifice, then honour is reprieved.

'To fight without hope is to fight with grace,
The self reconstructed, the false heart repaired.'
Then I turned with a smile, and he answered my salute
As he stood against the fretted hedge, which was like white
    lace.

from Ode Written during the Battle of Dunkirk, May 1940: II

The old guns
barked into my ear. Day and night
they shook the earth in which I cowered
or rained round me
detonations of steel and fire.

One of the dazed and disinherited
I crawled out of that mess
with two medals and a gift of blood-money.
No visible wounds to lick – only a resolve
to tell the truth without rhetoric

the truth about war and about men
involved in the indignities of war.

But the world was tired and would forget
forget the pain and squalor
forget the hunger and dread
forget the cry of those who died in agony
and the unbearable silence of those who suddenly
as we talked
fell sniped
with mouth still open and uncomprehending eyes.

*

It is right to forget
sights the mind cannot accommodate
terror that cannot be described
experience that cannot be exorcised in thought.

It is natural for others to resent
the parade of wounds
eyes haunted with unrevealed sorrows
the unholy pride of sacrifice.

Human, to relapse
into the old ways, to resume
the normality so patiently acquired
in days of peace.

And so we drifted twenty years
down the stream of time
feeling that such a storm
could not break again.

Feeling that our little house-boat was safe
until the last lock was reached.

Another twenty years
would see us home.

*

The day passes
the sun swerves
silently like a cyclist round the bend.
Disembodied voices drift past behind the hedge
the vespers of the blackbird and the thrush
rise and die. A golden frog
leaps out of the grasses.

In the silence of the twilight
I hear in the distance
the new guns.
I listen, no longer apt in war
unable to distinguish between bombs and shells.

As the evening deepens
searchlights begin to waver in the sky
the air-planes throb invisibly above me
There is still a glow in the west
and Venus shines brightly over the wooded hill.

Unreal war! No single friend
links me with its immediacy.
It is a voice out of a cabinet
a printed sheet, and these faint reverberations
selected in the silence
by my attentive ear.

Presently I shall sleep,
and sink into a deeper oblivion.

HENRY REED

Lessons of the War
To Alan Michell

Vixi duellis nuper idoneus
Et militavi non sine gloria

I NAMING OF PARTS

To-day we have naming of parts. Yesterday,
We had daily cleaning. And to-morrow morning,
We shall have what to do after firing. But to-day,
To-day we have naming of parts. Japonica
Glistens like coral in all of the neighbouring gardens,
     And to-day we have naming of parts.

This is the lower sling swivel. And this
Is the upper sling swivel, whose use you will see,
When you are given your slings. And this is the piling swivel,
Which in your case you have not got. The branches
Hold in the gardens their silent, eloquent gestures,
     Which in our case we have not got.

This is the safety-catch, which is always released
With an easy flick of the thumb. And please do not let me
See anyone using his finger. You can do it quite easy
If you have any strength in your thumb. The blossoms
Are fragile and motionless, never letting anyone see
     Any of them using their finger.

And this you can see is the bolt. The purpose of this
Is to open the breech, as you see. We can slide it
Rapidly backwards and forwards: we call this
Easing the spring. And rapidly backwards and forwards

The early bees are assaulting and fumbling the flowers:
   They call it easing the Spring.

They call it easing the Spring: it is perfectly easy
If you have any strength in your thumb: like the bolt,
And the breech, and the cocking-piece, and the point of
   balance,
Which in our case we have not got; and the almond-blossom
Silent in all of the gardens and the bees going backwards and
   forwards,
   For to-day we have naming of parts.

II JUDGING DISTANCES

Not only how far away, but the way that you say it
Is very important. Perhaps you may never get
The knack of judging a distance, but at least you know
How to report on a landscape: the central sector,
The right of arc and that, which we had last Tuesday,
   And at least you know

That maps are of time, not place, so far as the army
Happens to be concerned – the reason being,
Is one which need not delay us. Again, you know
There are three kinds of tree, three only, the fir and the
   poplar,
And those which have bushy tops to; and lastly
   That things only seem to be things.

A barn is not called a barn, to put it more plainly,
Or a field in the distance, where sheep may be safely grazing.
You must never be over-sure. You must say, when reporting:
At five o'clock in the central sector is a dozen
Of what appear to be animals; whatever you do,
   Don't call the bleeders *sheep*.

I am sure that's quite clear; and suppose, for the sake of
    example,
The one at the end, asleep, endeavours to tell us
What he sees over there to the west, and how far away,
After first having come to attention. There to the west,
On the fields of summer the sun and the shadows bestow
    Vestments of purple and gold.

The still white dwellings are like a mirage in the heat,
And under the swaying elms a man and a woman
Lie gently together. Which is, perhaps, only to say
That there is a row of houses to the left of arc,
And that under some poplars a pair of what appear to be
    humans
    Appear to be loving.

Well that, for an answer, is what we might rightly call
Moderately satisfactory only, the reason being,
Is that two things have been omitted, and those are
    important.
The human beings, now: in what direction are they,
And how far away, would you say? And do not forget
    There may be dead ground in between.

There may be dead ground in between; and I may not have
    got
The knack of judging a distance; I will only venture
A guess that perhaps between me and the apparent lovers,
(Who, incidentally, appear by now to have finished,)
At seven o'clock from the houses, is roughly a distance
    Of about one year and a half.

W. R. RODGERS

Stormy Day

O look how the loops and balloons of bloom
Bobbing on long strings from the finger-ends
And knuckles of the lurching cherry-tree
Heap and hug, elbow and part, this wild day,
Like a careless carillon cavorting;
And the beaded whips of the beeches splay
And dip like anchored weed round a drowned rock,
And hovering effortlessly the rooks
Hang on the wind's effrontery as if
On hooks, then loose their hold and slide away
Like sleet sidewards down the warm swimming sweep
Of wind. O it is a lovely time when
Out of the sunk and rigid sumps of thought
Our hearts rise and race with new sounds and sights
And signs, tingling delightedly at the sting
And crunch of springless carts on gritty roads,
The caught kite dangling in the skinny wires,
The swipe of a swallow across the eyes,
Striped awnings stretched on lawns. New things surprise
And stop us everywhere. In the parks
The fountains scoop and flower like rockets
Over the oval ponds whose even skin
Is pocked and goosefleshed by their niggling rain
That frocks a naked core of statuary.
And at jetty's jut, roped and ripe for hire,
The yellow boats lie yielding and lolling,
Jilted and jolted like jellies. But look!
There! Do you see, crucified on palings,

Motionless news-posters announcing
That now the frozen armies melt and meet
And smash? Go home now, for, try as you may,
You will not shake off that fact today.
Behind you limps that dog with tarry paw,
As behind him, perfectly timed, follows
The dumb shadow that mimes him all the way.

ALAN ROSS

Destroyers in the Arctic

Camouflaged, they detach lengths of sea and sky
When they move; offset, speed and direction are a lie.

Everything is grey anyway; ships, water, snow, faces.
Flanking the convoy, we rarely go through our paces:

But sometimes on tightening waves at night they wheel
Drawing white moons on strings from dripping keel.

Cold cases them, like ships in glass; they are formal,
Not real, except in adversity. Then, too, have to seem
    normal.

At dusk they intensify dusk, strung out, non-committal:
Waves spill from our wake, crêpe paper magnetised by gun-
    metal.

They breathe silence, less solid than ghosts, ruminative
As the Arctic breaks up on their sides and they sieve

Moisture into mess-decks. Heat is cold-lined there,
Where we wait for a torpedo and lack air.

Repetitive of each other, imitating the sea's lift and fall,
On the wings of the convoy they indicate rehearsal.

Merchantmen move sideways, with the gait of crustaceans,
Round whom like eels escorts take up their stations.

Landfall, Murmansk; but starboard now a lead-coloured
Island, Jan Mayen. Days identical, hoisted like sails, blurred.

Counters moved on an Admiralty map, snow like confetti
Covers the real us. We dream we are counterfeits tied to our
  jetty.

But cannot dream long; the sea curdles and sprawls,
Liverishly real, and merciless all else away from us falls.

TADEUSZ RÓŻEWICZ

The Survivor

I am twenty-four
led to slaughter
I survived.

The following are empty synonyms:
man and beast
love and hate
friend and foe
darkness and light.

The way of killing men and beasts is the same
I've seen it:
truckfuls of chopped-up men
who will not be saved.

Ideas are mere words:
virtue and crime
truth and lies
beauty and ugliness
courage and cowardice.

Virtue and crime weigh the same
I've seen it:
in a man who was both
criminal and virtuous.

I seek a teacher and a master
may he restore my sight hearing and speech
may he again name objects and ideas
may he separate darkness from light.

I am twenty-four
led to slaughter
I survived.

Translated from the Polish by Adam Czerniawski

The Return

Suddenly the window will open
and mother will call
it's time to come in

the wall will part
I will enter heaven in muddy shoes

I will come to the table
and answer questions rudely

I am all right leave me
alone. Head in hand I
sit and sit. How can I tell them
about that long
and tangled way.

Here in heaven mothers
knit green scarves

flies buzz

father dozes by the stove
after six days' labour.

No – surely I can't tell them
that men are at each
other's throats.

Translated by Adam Czerniawski

Abattoirs

Pink quartered ideals
hang in abattoirs

Shops are selling
clowns'
motley death-masks
stripped off the faces
of us who live
who have survived
staring
into the eye-socket of war.

Translated by Adam Czerniawski

Pigtail

When all the women in the transport
had their heads shaved
four workmen with brooms made of birch twigs
swept up
and gathered up the hair

Behind clean glass
the stiff hair lies
of those suffocated in gas chambers
there are pins and side combs
in this hair

The hair is not shot through with light
is not parted by the breeze
is not touched by any hand
or rain or lips

In huge chests
clouds of dry hair
of those suffocated
and a faded plait
a pigtail with a ribbon
pulled at school
by naughty boys.

The Museum, Auschwitz, 1948

Translated by Adam Czerniawski

Massacre of the Boys

The children cried 'Mummy!
But I have been good!
It's dark in here! Dark!'

See them They are going to the bottom
See the small feet
they went to the bottom Do you see
that print
of a small foot here and there

pockets bulging
with string and stones
and little horses made of wire

A great closed plain
like a figure of geometry
and a tree of black smoke
a vertical

dead tree
with no star in its crown.

The Museum, Auschwitz, 1948

Translated by Adam Czerniawski

NELLY SACHS

O the chimneys
And though after my skin worms destroy this
body, yet in my flesh shall I see God.

Job, 19:26

O the chimneys
On the ingeniously devised habitations of death
When Israel's body drifted as smoke
Through the air –
Was welcomed by a star, a chimney sweep,
A star that turned black
Or was it a ray of sun?

O the chimneys!
Freedomway for Jeremiah and Job's dust –
Who devised you and laid stone upon stone
The road for refugees of smoke?

O the habitations of death,
Invitingly appointed
For the host who used to be a guest –
O you fingers
Laying the threshold
Like a knife between life and death –

O you chimneys,
O you fingers
And Israel's body as smoke through the air!

Translated from the German by Michael Roloff

O the night of the weeping children!

O the night of the weeping children!
O the night of the children branded for death!
Sleep may not enter here.
Terrible nursemaids
Have usurped the place of mothers,
Have tautened their tendons with the false death,
Sow it on to the walls and into the beams –
Everywhere it is hatched in the nests of horror.
Instead of mother's milk, panic suckles those little ones.

Yesterday Mother still drew
Sleep toward them like a white moon,
There was the doll with cheeks derouged by kisses
In one arm,
The stuffed pet, already
Brought to life by love,
In the other –
Now blows the wind of dying,
Blows the shifts over the hair
That no one will comb again.

Translated by Michael Hamburger

What secret cravings of the blood

What secret cravings of the blood,
Dreams of madness and earth
A thousand times murdered,
Brought into being the terrible puppeteer?

Him who with foaming mouth
Dreadfully swept away

The round, the circling stage of his deed
With the ash-grey, receding horizon of fear?

O the hills of dust, which as though drawn by an evil moon
The murderers enacted:

Arms up and down,
Legs up and down
And the setting sun of Sinai's people
A red carpet under their feet.

Arms up and down,
Legs up and down
And on the ash-grey receding horizon of fear
Gigantic the constellation of death
That loomed like the clock face of ages.

Translated by Michael Hamburger

Numbers

When your forms turned to ashes
into the oceans of night
where eternity washes
life and death into the tides –

there rose the numbers –
(once branded into your arms
so none would escape the agony)

there rose meteors of numbers
beckoned into the spaces
where light-years expand like arrows
and the pianets
are born
of the magic substances of pain –

[246]

numbers – root and all
plucked out of murderers' brains
and part already
of the heavenly cycle's
path of blue veins.

Translated by Michael Roloff

The Myth of Hiroshima

What are they looking for,
running to the summit of lost time?
Hundreds of people vaporised instantly
are walking in mid-air.

    'We didn't die.'
    'We skipped over death in a flash and became spirits.'
    'Give us a real, human death.'

One man's shadow among hundreds is branded on stone
    steps.

    'Why am I imprisoned in stone?'
    'Where did my flesh go, separated from its shadow?'
    'What must I wait for?'

The twentieth century myth is stamped with fire.
Who will free this shadow from the stone?

Translated from the Japanese by Hajime Kajima

KURT SCHWITTERS

Flight

The Germans are coming –
The Germans?
Here in Norway?
30 bombers flying over –
Is it war?
The airplane down in flames –
Woods burning –
A machine gun –
Radio? So soon?
They've taken Bergen, Trondheim –
Aalesund?
Still free –
And Narvik?
What do the Germans want here?
To help Norway –
Got to pack our things –
Everyone into the cellar –
Got to pack –
You've got to go into the cellar –
Packing –
Too damn dangerous –
What is this life about?
Into the cellar –
No, to freedom.
Where?
Where?
Anywhere but here –
Did you see the airplane burning?

Dogfight over Oslo –
War all right –
That started it –
Attacking a free country –
They just want to help –
No, I don't get it –
We've got to start in packing –
Take just what you need!
Did you hear the machine gun?
Don't leave out your toothbrush –
And the paints –
I'm taking something I can paint with –
They'll be out again soon –
England's helping –
You won't get a chance to paint –
Pack real good –
That lovely freshly painted floor! –
We can't clean up here any more –
They'll be here any time now –
The shooting's ended out in Fornebu –
The wounded are down at the hotel –
We better get a move on –
Pay the the 2 months rent up front!
Go easy, Herr Jensen, you've got no cause to worry –
Well, just don't look back!
We'll be back here in 8 days –
There's no car to be had –
All cars are being used for the evacuation –
Not something you could lend us? –
Take our wheelbarrow!
That gunfire's something awful –
Hurry up, they're shooting from the airplanes!
I'll be going back and forth –

When you get back, we'll have some coffee –
With all of those machine guns –
Hope it goes real well, Frau Jensen!
See you soon, goodbye, take care!
I'll get the wheelbarrow at the station –
They're shooting at us from the airplanes!
Put the bags under the roof!
There, there in the wall, the bullets are hitting –
Here comes the airplane a third time!
No real damage –
But the train looks jammed!
We must be out of their line of fire –
How calm the fjord is in the snow –
Good the three of us are here together –
Tomorrow would have been too late for Esther –
We'll take an auto to the east bahnhof –
No more autos!
Streetcar isn't running –
Electricity's cut off –
We can't carry all this luggage!
Should have filled our papers out beforehand!
Didn't have the time –
What if our records are destroyed?
We ought to stop a passing auto!
There's one coming now!
It's all of the people from the station!
I know a side door there: 'Off Limits'! –
If you just know how to go about it . . .
Or else we wouldn't have gotten to the platform –
Good thing the train is running late.
Here it comes now!
Beg your pardon, did I bump you?
There's my third suitcase over there! – – Oh thanks.

Won't you let the old lady sit down?
Oh sure.
Here comes a woman with a baby!
Give her your seat! – – –
Air raid siren.
Well it's finally gotten going! –
Did you see the soldiers in the woods there?
And the snow!
I can still get another postcard off to Helma.
It'll get through.

Translated from the German by Jerome Rothenberg
and Pierre Joris

E. J. SCOVELL

Days Drawing In

The days fail: night broods over afternoon:
And at my child's first drink beyond the night
Her skin is silver in the early light.
Sweet the grey morning and the raiders gone.

Daylight Alert

When the daylight Alert has sounded, calling us
To what? not fear but application – we seemed to have
    stepped across
A line in time, like a low wall that nettles guard,
Into a place marked off, an orchard or unkept graveyard.

The long gust sinks to peace, children who cried recover
Their joy; we stand in grass and look, the low wall is crossed
    over.
This is another realm where silence is loud,
The sun shines so, the grass springs thicker, the fruits rush
    and thud.

Bombs have not fallen on our town; the shoppers scarcely
Lift eyes to the clear sky and fighters crossing straight and
    sparsely.
Our blood no more than smiles at this *memento mori*
As if it were a skull in flowers or a pale murder story.

Only our souls say in the stillness of their breath:
This is the hour that may be ours, the hour of pain and
    death.

What are we waiting for? What are stretched to meet
Here in a walled and haunted plot set in our shopping
    street?

The hour shuts like a flower or dream when it is ended,
The far wall come upon too suddenly, the All Clear sounded.
It was not death but life we were to entertain,
Waving to one who flashed so fast by in a royal train;

Called not to death but thought, still called to application,
Standing with empty eyes, dropped hands, at the small
    railway station,
On the flowered country platform, we who have come so far
To honour one we never meet – wind, is he? falling star?

GEORGE SEFERIS

Last Stop

Few are the moonlit nights that I've cared for:
the alphabet of the stars – which you spell out
as much as your fatigue at the day's end allows
and from which you gather other meanings and other
    hopes –
you can then read more clearly.
Now that I sit here, idle, and think about it,
few are the moons that remain in my memory:
islands, color of grieving Madonna, late in the waning
or moonlight in northern cities sometimes casting
over turbulent streets, rivers, and limbs of men
a heavy torpor.
Yet here last evening, in this our final port
where we wait for the hour of our return home to dawn
like an old debt: money that lay for years
in a miser's safe, and at last
the time for payment comes
and you hear the coins falling onto the table;
in this Etruscan village, behind the sea of Salerno
behind the harbors of our return, on the edge
of an autumn squall, the moon
outstripped the clouds, and houses
on the slope opposite became enamel:
Amica silentia lunae.

This is a train of thought, a way
to begin to speak of things you confess
uneasily, at times when you can't hold back, to a friend

who escaped secretly and who brings
word from home and from the companions,
and you hurry to open your heart
before this exile forestalls you and alters him.
We come from Arabia, Egypt, Palestine, Syria;
the little state
of Kommagene, which flickered out like a small lamp,
often comes to mind,
and great cities that lived for thousands of years
and then became pasture land for cattle,
fields for sugar-cane and corn.
We come from the sand of the desert, from the seas of
    Proteus,
souls shriveled by public sins,
each holding office like a bird in its cage.
The rainy autumn in this gorge
infects the wound of each of us
or what you might term differently: nemesis, fate,
or simply bad habits, fraud and deceit,
or even the selfish urge to reap reward from the blood of
    others.
Man frays easily in wars;
man is soft, a sheaf of grass,
lips and fingers that hunger for a white breast
eyes that half-close in the radiance of day
and feet that would run, no matter how tired,
at the slightest call of profit.
Man is soft and thirsty like grass,
insatiable like grass, his nerves roots that spread;
when the harvest comes
he would rather have the scythes whistle in some other field;
when the harvest comes
some call out to exorcise the demon

some become entangled in their riches, others deliver
    speeches.
But what good are exorcisms, riches, speeches
when the living are far away?
Is man ever anything else?
Isn't it this that confers life?
A time for planting, a time for harvesting.

'The same thing over and over again,' you'll tell me, friend.
But the thinking of a refugee, the thinking of a prisoner, the
    thinking
of a person when he too has become a commodity –
try to change it; you can't.
Maybe he would have liked to stay king of the cannibals
wasting strength that nobody buys,
to promenade in fields of agapanthi
to hear the drums with bamboo overhead,
as courtiers dance with prodigious masks.
But the country they're chopping up and burning like a pine-
    tree – you see it
either in the dark train, without water, the windows broken,
    night after night
or in the burning ship that according to the statistics is
    bound to sink –
this has taken root in the mind and doesn't change
this has planted images like those trees
that cast their branches in virgin forests
so that they take root in the earth and sprout again;
they cast their branches that sprout again, striding mile after
    mile;
our mind's a virgin forest of murdered friends.
And if I talk to you in fables and parables
it's because it's more gentle for you that way; and horror

really can't be talked about because it's alive,
because it's mute and goes on growing:
memory-wounding pain
drips by day drips in sleep.

To speak of heroes to speak of heroes: Michael
who left the hospital with his wounds still open,
maybe he was speaking of heroes – the night
he dragged his foot through the darkened city –
when he howled, groping over our pain: 'We advance in the
    dark,
we move forward in the dark . . .'
The heroes move forward in the dark.

Few are the moonlit nights that I've cared for.

Cava dei Tirreni, 5 October 1944

*Translated from the Greek by Edmund Keeley
and Philip Sherrard*

Never Again

A hundred houses were in ruins,
nearly a thousand had been damaged
by aerial bombs.
No, I didn't count them myself.
I worked my way through the rubble
and circumnavigated the craters.
They were frightening
like gaping gates to fiery hell.

Speedily they cleared away the debris
but it was three days before
they broke into the little house
in Šverma Street,
the house of Mr Hrnčíř.
The whole family was dead.

Only the rooster, that fighting cock
whom the Apostle Peter did not
greatly love,
alone had saved himself.
Over the bodies of the dead he'd climbed
onto a pile of rubble.

He looked about the scene of the disaster
and spread his wings
to shake the heavy dust
from his golden feathers.

And I repeated softly to myself
what I had found written

in letters of grief and in letters of pain
upon the faces of the Kralupy people.

And into that silence of death
I screamed in a loud voice,
so loud the war should hear it:
Never again, war!

The rooster looked at me
with its black beady eye
and burst into horrible laughter.
He laughed at me
and at my pointless screaming.
Besides, he was a bird
and sided with the planes.
The bastard!

Translated from the Czech by Ewald Osers

LOUIS SIMPSON

The Battle

Helmet and rifle, pack and overcoat
Marched through a forest. Somewhere up ahead
Guns thudded. Like the circle of a throat
The night on every side was turning red.

They halted and they dug. They sank like moles
Into the clammy earth between the trees.
And soon the sentries, standing in their holes,
Felt the first snow. Their feet began to freeze.

At dawn the first shell landed with a crack.
Then shells and bullets swept the icy woods.
This lasted many days. The snow was black.
The corpses stiffened in their scarlet hoods.

Most clearly of that battle I remember
The tiredness in eyes, how hands looked thin
Around a cigarette, and the bright ember
Would pulse with all the life there was within.

Carentan O Carentan

Trees in the old days used to stand
And shape a shady lane
Where lovers wandered hand in hand
Who came from Carentan.

This was the shining green canal
Where we came two by two

Walking at combat-interval.
Such trees we never knew.

The day was early June, the ground
Was soft and bright with dew.
Far away the guns did sound,
But here the sky was blue.

The sky was blue, but there a smoke
Hung still above the sea
Where the ships together spoke
To towns we could not see.

Could you have seen us through a glass
You would have said a walk
Of farmers out to turn the grass,
Each with his own hay-fork.

The watchers in their leopard suits
Waited till it was time,
And aimed between the belt and boot
And let the barrel climb.

I must lie down at once, there is
A hammer at my knee.
And call it death or cowardice,
Don't count again on me.

Everything's all right, Mother,
Everyone gets the same
At one time or another.
It's all in the game.

I never strolled, nor ever shall,
Down such a leafy lane.
I never drank in a canal,
Nor ever shall again.

There is a whistling in the leaves
And it is not the wind,
The twigs are falling from the knives
That cut men to the ground.

Tell me, Master-Sergeant,
The way to turn and shoot.
But the Sergeant's silent
That taught me how to do it.

O Captain, show us quickly
Our place upon the map.
But the Captain's sickly
And taking a long nap.

Lieutenant, what's my duty,
My place in the platoon?
He too's a sleeping beauty,
Charmed by that strange tune.

Carentan O Carentan
Before we met with you
We never yet had lost a man
Or known what death could do.

A Story about Chicken Soup

In my grandmother's house there was always chicken soup
And talk of the old country – mud and boards,
Poverty,
The snow falling down the necks of lovers.

Now and then, out of her savings
She sent them a dowry. Imagine

The rice-powdered faces!
And the smell of the bride, like chicken soup.

But the Germans killed them.
I know it's in bad taste to say it,
But it's true. The Germans killed them all.

*

In the ruins of Berchtesgaden
A child with yellow hair
Ran out of a doorway.

A German girl-child –
Cuckoo, all skin and bones –
Not even enough to make chicken soup.
She sat by the stream and smiled.

Then as we splashed in the sun
She laughed at us.
We had killed her mechanical brothers,
So we forgave her.

*

The sun is shining.
The shadows of the lovers have disappeared.
They are all eyes; they have some demand on me –
They want me to be more serious than I want to be.

They want me to stick in their mudhole
Where no one is elegant.
They want me to wear old clothes,
They want me to be poor, to sleep in a room with many
   others –

Not to walk in the painted sunshine
To a summer house,
But to live in the tragic world forever.

KENNETH SLESSOR

An Inscription for Dog River

Our general was the greatest and bravest of generals.
For his deeds, look around you on this coast –
Here is his name cut next to Ashur-Bani-Pal's,
Nebuchadnezzar's and the Roman host;
And we, though our identities have been lost,
Lacking the validity of stone or metal,
We, too, are part of his memorial,
Having been put in for the cost,

Having bestowed on him all we had to give
In battles few can recollect,
Our strength, obedience and endurance,
Our wits, our bodies, our existence,
Even our descendants' right to live –
Having given him everything, in fact,
Except respect.

Beach Burial

Softly and humbly to the Gulf of Arabs
The convoys of dead sailors come;
At night they sway and wander in the waters far under,
But morning rolls them in the foam.

Between the sob and clubbing of the gunfire
Someone, it seems, has time for this,
To pluck them from the shallows and bury them in burrows
And tread the sand upon their nakedness;

And each cross, the driven stake of tidewood,
Bears the last signature of men,
Written with such perplexity, with such bewildered pity,
The words choke as they begin –

'*Unknown seaman*' – the ghostly pencil
Wavers and fades, the purple drips,
The breath of the wet season has washed their inscriptions
As blue as drowned men's lips,

Dead seamen, gone in search of the same landfall,
Whether as enemies they fought,
Or fought with us, or neither; the sand joins them together,
Enlisted on the other front.

El Alamein

BORIS SLUTSKY

My Friends

My friends in tanks were burnt
to cinders, to ashes, to dust.
Grass, covering half a world,
has grown out of them of course.
My friends,
          stumbling onto mines,
took off upwards,
               were blown sky high,
and lots of peaceful, distant stars
from them,
       from my friends,
              caught fire.
People recount their deeds on public holidays,
make films out of them for show,
and my fellow students, my classmates,
turned into verse long ago.

Translated from the Russian by Daniel Weissbort

El Alamein

O, dearlie they deed
St Valery's vengers
– The gleds dine weel
In the Libyan desert –
Dearlie they deed,
Aa the winds furthtell it.

Around El Alamein
Ranks o carrion
Faur frae their hame
Ligg sterk in the sun,
In the rutted sand
Whaur the tanks has run.

Yon burnan daw
Than dumb-deid blacker,
Whiter than snaw
Will the bricht banes glitter;
That this was for Alba
Maun we mak siccar!

It wasna for thraldom
Ye ligg there deid,
Gin we should fail ye
The rocks wad bleed!
– O, the gleds foregaither
Roun Alba's deid.

gleds, kites; *Ligg sterk*, lie stark; *burnan daw*, burning dawn;
dumb-deid, dead of night; *banes*, bones; *Alba*, Scotland; *maun*,
must; *siccar*, sure

The Mither's Lament

Whit care I for the leagues o sand,
The prisoners an the gear theyve won?
Ma darlin liggs amang the dunes
Wi mony a mither's son.

Doutless he deed for Scotland's life;
Doutless the statesmen dinna lee;
But och tis sair begrutten pride
An wersh the wine o victorie!

lee, lie; *begrutten*, lamented; *wersh*, sour

STEVIE SMITH

Voices against England in the Night

'England, you had better go,
There is nothing else that you ought to do,
You lump of survival value, you are too slow.

England, you have been here too long,
And the songs you sing are the songs you sung
On a braver day. Now they are wrong.

And as you sing the sliver slips from your lips,
And the governing garments sits ridiculously on your hips.
It is a pity that you are still too cunning to make slips.'

Dr Goebbels, that is the point,
You are a few years too soon with your jaunt,
Time and the moment is not yet England's daunt.

Yes, dreaming Germany with your Urge and Night,
You must go down before English and American might.
It is well, it is well, cries the peace kite.

Perhaps England our darling will recover her lost thought
We must think sensibly about our victory and not be
    distraught,
Perhaps America will have an idea, and perhaps not.

But they cried: Could not England, once the world's best,
Put off her governing garment and be better dressed
In a shroud, a shroud? O history turn thy pages fast!

The Poets are Silent

There's no new spirit abroad,
As I looked, I saw;
And I say that it is to the poets' merit
To be silent about the war.

I Remember

It was my bridal night I remember,
an old man of seventy-three
I lay with my young bride in my arms,
A girl with t.b.
It was war-time, and overhead
The Germans were making a particularly heavy raid on
    Hampstead.
What rendered the confusion worse, perversely
Our bombers had chosen that moment to set out for
    Germany.
Harry, do they ever collide?
I do not think it has ever happened,
Oh my bride, my bride.

BERNARD SPENCER

Salonika June 1940

My end of Europe is at war. For this
My lamp-launched giant shadow seems to fall
Like a bad thought upon this ground at peace,
Being the shadow of the shadow of a war.
What difference if I wish good luck to these foreigners, my
    hosts?
Talking with my friends stand ghosts.

Specially the lives that here in the crook of this bay
At the paws of its lionish hills are lived as I know;
The dancing, the bathing, the order of the market, and as
    day
Cools into night, boys playing in the square;
Island boats and lemon-peel tang and the timeless café
    crowd,
And the outcry of dice on wood:

I would shut the whole if I could out of harm's way
As one shuts a holiday photo away in a desk,
Or shuts one's eyes. But not by this brilliant bay,
Nor in Hampstead now where leaves are green,
Any more exists a word or a lock which gunfire may not
    break,
Or a love whose range it may not take.

FRANZ BAERMANN STEINER

8th May 1945

Hasty is the flight of birds. Woe, all that was ever ready to
    soar
Has the weight of stones
That endure under the earth, cemented with the bodies and
    years of love.

People have buried their wickedly pampered war.
Poppies bloom out of beer.
Paper-chains lace up the bodies of feverish houses.

The wet flags drip into sultry, festive air.
Behind the roll of drums
A skater zigzags over a frozen lake of blood.

Translated from the German by Michael Hamburger

WALLACE STEVENS

Man and Bottle

The mind is the great poem of winter, the man,
Who, to find what will suffice,
Destroys romantic tenements
Of rose and ice

In the land of war. More than the man, it is
A man with the fury of a race of men,
A light at the centre of many lights,
A man at the centre of men.

It has to content the reason concerning war,
It has to persuade that war is part of itself,
A manner of thinking, a mode
Of destroying, as the mind destroys,

An aversion, as the world is averted
From an old delusion, an old affair with the sun,
An impossible aberration with the moon,
A grossness of peace.

It is not the snow that is the quill, the page.
The poem lashes more fiercely than the wind,
As the mind, to find what will suffice, destroys
Romantic tenements of rose and ice.

Martial Cadenza

I

Only this evening I saw again low in the sky
The evening star, at the beginning of winter, the star
That in spring will crown every western horizon,
Again . . . as if it came back, as if life came back,
Not in a later son, a different daughter, another place,
But as if evening found us young, still young,
Still walking in a present of our own.

II

It was like sudden time in a world without time,
This world, this place, the street in which I was,
Without time: as that which is not has no time,
Is not, or is of what there was, is full
Of the silence before the armies, armies without
Either trumpets or drums, the commanders mute, the arms
On the ground, fixed fast in a profound defeat.

III

What had this star to do with the world it lit,
With the blank skies over England, over France
And above the German camps? It looked apart.
Yet it is this that shall maintain – Itself
Is time, apart from any past, apart
From any future, the ever-living and being,
The ever-breathing and moving, the constant fire,

IV

The present close, the present realised,
Not the symbol but that for which the symbol stands,

The vivid thing in the air that never changes,
Though the air change. Only this evening I saw it again,
At the beginning of winter, and I walked and talked
Again, and lived and was again, and breathed again
And moved again and flashed again, time flashed again.

LEON ZDZISŁAW STROIŃSKI

Warsaw

During the building of the barricades, the Vistula, brimming with reflections of forests, birds and white roads lined with poplars, rose, at first like a mist, then like a stiff cover of a book.

In its shade at dawn caretakers come out with huge frayed brooms to sweep up the tears which have collected during the night and lie thickly in the streets.

Already, the market women, extended to the edge of the sunlight, recommend potatoes grown on graves.

And on the horizon of the street, across the roar of grenades lying in the curves of cobblestones, the soul of the city has been moving for months.

The reflection of her face, too difficult to comprehend, has left a trace on the twisted faces of ruins as on the handkerchief of St Veronica.

Those who will come in the far, far future wanting to decipher them, drawing their cold-blue hands across features taut like strings, and who with careless fingers will poke the moan of those dried up in crevices –

will burst into prayer or blasphemy.

Here my country has come together from decimated forests and villages turned into a dog's howl. It persists in the whisper of mechanised armour.

We had to wait through so much blood and pathos in order to build from the silence of ruined monuments such a vault over a city of jazz and death.

Now lemurs from Gothic temples are thick on roofs of trams and terrify insurance officials on their way home.

[278]

The dead wander beneath the pavements and pound on bucklers which give a hollow sound, while at evening in double rows of whispers they walk arm in arm with the living, and you can tell them apart only by the skilfully folded wings, which nevertheless stick out on their backs like humps.

But in daytime huge stone capstans hum, and only around noon, when folk sit down to lunch and it's a bit quieter, can you hear more distinctly the heavy rhythmical tread of God's steel-shod boots.

Translated from the Polish by Adam Czerniawski

ANNA SWIRSZCYŃSKA

He Was Lucky
To Prof. Wladyslaw Tatarkiewicz

The old man
leaves his house, carries books.
A German soldier snatches the books
flings them in the mud.

The old man picks them up,
the soldier hits him in the face.

The old man falls,
the soldier kicks him and walks away.

The old man
lies in mud and blood.
Under him he feels
the books.

*Translated from the Polish by Magnus Jan Krynski
and Robert Maguire*

Building the Barricade

We were afraid as we built the barricade
under fire.

The tavern-keeper, the jeweller's mistress, the barber,
all of us cowards.

The servant-girl fell to the ground
as she lugged a paving stone, we were terribly afraid

[280]

all of us cowards –
the janitor, the market-woman, the pensioner.

The pharmacist fell to the ground
as he dragged the door of a toilet,
we were even more afraid, the smuggler-woman,
the dressmaker, the streetcar driver,
all of us cowards.

A kid from reform school fell
as he dragged a sandbag,
you see we were really
afraid.

Though no one forced us,
we did build the barricade
under fire.

Translated by Magnus Jan Krynski and Robert Maguire

HARA TAMIKI

'In the fire, a telegraph pole'

In the fire, a telegraph pole
At the heart of the fire.
A telegraph pole like a stamen,
Like a candle,
Blazing up, like a molten
Red stamen.
In the heart of the fire on the other bank
From this morning, one by one,
Fear has screamed
Through men's eyes. At the heart of the fire
A telegraph pole, like a stamen.

*Translated from the Japanese by Geoffrey Bownas
and Anthony Thwaite*

Glittering fragments

Glittering fragments
Ashen embers
Like a rippling panorama,
Burning red then dulled.
Strange rhythm of human corpses.
All existence, all that could exist
Laid bare in a flash. The rest of the world
The swelling of a horse's corpse
At the side of an upturned train,
The smell of smouldering electric wires.

Translated by Geoffrey Bownas and Anthony Thwaite

DYLAN THOMAS

Deaths and Entrances

On almost the incendiary eve
   Of several near deaths,
When one at the great least of your best loved
   And always known must leave
Lions and fires of his flying breath,
   Of your immortal friends
Who'd raise the organs of the counted dust
   To shoot and sing your praise,
One who called deepest down shall hold his peace
   That cannot sink or cease
   Endlessly to his wound
In many married London's estranging grief.

On almost the incendiary eve
   When at your lips and keys,
Locking, unlocking, the murdered strangers weave,
   One who is most unknown,
Your polestar neighbour, sun of another street,
   Will dive up to his tears.
He'll bathe his raining blood in the male sea
   Who strode for your own dead
And wind his globe out of your water thread
   And load the throats of shells
   With every cry since light
Flashed first across his thunderclapping eyes.

On almost the incendiary eve
   Of deaths and entrances,
When near and strange wounded on London's waves

Have sought your single grave,
One enemy, of many, who knows well
    Your heart is luminous
In the watched dark, quivering through locks and caves,
    Will pull the thunderbolts
To shut the sun, plunge, mount your darkened keys
    And sear just riders back,
    Until that one loved least
Looms the last Samson of your zodiac.

A Refusal to Mourn the Death, by Fire, of a Child in London

Never until the mankind making
Bird beast and flower
Fathering and all humbling darkness
Tells with silence the last light breaking
And the still hour
Is come of the sea tumbling in harness

And I must enter again the round
Zion of the water bead
And the synagogue of the ear of corn
Shall I let pray the shadow of a sound
Or sow my salt seed
In the least valley of sackcloth to mourn

The majesty and burning of the child's death.
I shall not murder
The mankind of her going with a grave truth
Nor blaspheme down the stations of the breath
With any further
Elegy of innocence and youth.

Deep with the first dead lies London's daughter,
Robed in the long friends,
The grains beyond age, the dark veins of her mother,
Secret by the unmourning water
Of the riding Thames.
After the first death, there is no other.

RUTH TOMALIN

Embroidery, 1940

The day the shattered Germans lay in shreds
among the placid nettles at the gate,
I took a skein of sunset-coloured threads
to make my brave Red Admiral a mate.

When snarling dog-fights trailed across the blue,
and men went home at night to count their dead,
over the gold-eyed purple iris flew
a Tiger Moth in goblin green and red.

I cannot see the Painted Lady's wings,
embroidered apricot and veined in buff,
without remembering quite other things
that happened while the land-mines did their stuff.

'England can take it!' runs the gallant line:
and later, as we gossip of the blitz,
we shall imagine everyone felt fine,
just waiting to be blown to little bits.

We may forget; but here they testify
the passive agony of long suspense –
the rose, the orchid and the butterfly:
good Lord deliver us from that pretence!

The sickening dive of planes, the dripping glass,
the bloody fire-bomb singing to the kill,
are sewn in delicate bright wings and grass,
and writ, in satin-stitch, upon the squill.

Objects

I am deeply convinced that objects
Are more eloquent than words . . .

Here is the bell that summoned the weavers
Furriers and tinsmiths to the *veche*.

Here is the bugle the Jacobins sounded
To herald the ending of the age of evil.

And here is the poker with which
They stirred the white ash in Auschwitz.

Translated from the Russian by Daniel Weissbort

Adam

On the first day, gazing idly about him,
He trampled the grass down and stretched himself
In the shade of the fig tree.
                              And placing

His hands behind his head,
                              he dozed.

Sweetly he slept, his sleep was untroubled,
In Eden's quiet, beneath the pale blue sky.
And in his dreams he saw the ovens of Auschwitz
And ditches filled with corpses.

He saw his own children!
                              In the bliss

Of paradise, his face lit up.
He slept, understanding nothing,
Not knowing good and evil yet.

Translated by Daniel Weissbort

ALEKSANDER WAT

To a Roman, My Friend

Everything that lies in rubble
reaches tenderly at me:
the ruins of my Warsaw
the ruins of your Rome.

In April 'forty-six
I saw two old goats
searching for some special herbs
in the former Albrecht's Café
(now overgrown with nettles,
thistles, burdock, spear grass).
Their barefoot shepherdess
in graveyard stillness
stood gaping, a child, under a pathetic column that once
     adorned the fourth floor
                              of the Credit Society building,
where then it was just a fancy ornament
changed today into an orphaned pendicle
on a fragment of charred wall.

On the Aventino I met two goats, roamers of ruins,
and a barefoot shepherdess
staring at faded frescoes.

Thus after man's glory,
after his acts and disasters
goats arrive. Smelly,
comic and worthy goats
to search among remnants of glory

for medicinal herbs and forage
for earthly nourishment.

*Translated from the Polish by Czeslaw Miłosz
and Leonard Nathan*

To Paul Éluard

Leaves whirl, leaves swirl,
leaves torn from Auschwitz trees.
Leaves in a gold-gray windstorm
leaves torn off leaves stripped off
leaves hacked flogged
gassed charred
leaves kneeling leaves screaming
leaves raising a lament to heaven!

My eyes stricken by terrible leaves,
they confuse my steps, turn me
they turn and darken, leaves, leaves
till I fall down
tangled in leaves
in leafing darkness!

Oh, close your eyes, sleepy Kore
who repose on your bed,
flayed and bloodless.
O lute of my sighs, be silent, be silent!
O close your eyes, buried
by leaves from Auschwitz.

April 1946

Translated by Czeslaw Miłosz and Leonard Nathan

An Attempt to Describe the Last Skirmish
of the Second World war
(A scenario of a dream)

To My Brother

Moonlight. Middle of summer. Stench of corpses.
I am walking through a burned-out city. Wroclaw.
I scare away a pack of rats. Of dogs. I enter
a wide prospect. And no living soul.
Even the vermin have established their quarters elsewhere.
I push through tall weeds,
and the night is lit by the moon: Luna, white, full. On both
sides two rows of houses
burned out inside. Only their blackened fronts
stand, indifferent. And the gypsum of stucco whitens,
strangely human, the white like the thigh
of an old woman. As Artemis, silvery,
stood above my head, I hear:
in front of me two boots approach,
they clatter, hobnailed,
on the granite squares of the pavement, though the street
is overgrown with nettles. In moonlight, soldier's
boots, without laces, wide toecaps, leather
well shined but vamps rotten,
with cracks, like a stonecutter's hand,
size twelve, for flat, thick-skinned feet.
(I repeat: No living soul! Not even a fly!)
I imagine their wearer: his weight, height,
his jaw . . . To meet him here! I trembled, completely soaked,
while the boots marched to me. Half an inch from me
they swerve, suddenly, incredibly deft.
They bypassed me. Went farther. Out of fright

throwing back my head, I started to bark at Hecate.
Which, pure, also moved away in the other,
opposite direction . . . The boots, stopped. Hesitant. Then
a rustling of plants parted in silent night.
O Lavanah! Oh, I have never seen her so beautiful: Above
 the horizon –
for now, before dawn, the prospect's end is visible: a gentle
 outline
        of mountains.
Not white, nor silvery, the very essence of light, in its perfect
 roundness,
she, immaculate. And there one star, her servant-maid,
 faithful.
She descends slowly, slowly, weighed down by its perfection.
 I weep
raising my hands toward her: O Lady of Biblos, I have
 always been
your loyal worshipper, have pity on me.
And the boots march, they won't ever abandon me: a couple
 of prisoners
behind the last warrior of the world war that is the last.
They follow me everywhere.
On my grave they, too, perhaps will bark? To Tanit?
If she shines for me: much is my hope.
What could I do without hope?

Translated by Czeslaw Miłosz and Leonard Nathan

FRANCIS WEBB

The Gunner

When the gunner spoke in his sleep the hut was still,
Uneasily strapped to the reckless wheel of his will;
Silence, humble, directionless as fog,
Lifted, and minutes were rhythmical on the log;

While slipstream plucked at a wafer of glass and steel,
Engines sliced and scooped at the air's thin wall,
And those dim spars dislodged from the moon became
Red thongs of tracer whipping boards aflame.

Listening, you crouched in the turret, watchful and taut
– *Bogey two thousand, skipper, corkscrew to port* –
Marvellous, the voice: driving electric fires
Through the panel of sleep, the black plugs, trailing wires.

The world spoke through its dream, being deaf and blind,
Its words were those of the dream, yet you might find
Forgotten genius, control, alive in this deep
Instinctive resistance to the perils of sleep.

First Snow in Alsace

The snow came down last night like moths
Burned on the moon; it fell till dawn,
Covered the town with simple cloths.

Absolute snow lies rumpled on
What shellbursts scattered and deranged,
Entangled railings, crevassed lawn.

As if it did not know they'd changed,
Snow smoothly clasps the roofs of homes
Fear-gutted, trustless and estranged.

The ration stacks are milky domes;
Across the ammunition pile
The snow has climbed in sparkling combs.

You think: beyond the town a mile
Or two, this snowfall fills the eyes
Of soldiers dead a little while.

Persons and persons in disguise,
Walking the new air white and fine,
Trade glances quick with shared surprise.

At children's windows, heaped, benign,
As always, winter shines the most,
And frost makes marvelous designs.

The night guard coming from his post,
Ten first-snows back in thought, walks slow
And warms him with a boyish boast:

He was the first to see the snow.

[294]

Potato

for André du Bouchet

An underground grower, blind and a common brown;
Got a misshapen look, it's nudged where it could;
Simple as soil yet crowded as earth with all.

Cut open raw, it looses a cool clean stench,
Mineral acid seeping from pores of prest meal;
It is like breaching a strangely refreshing tomb:

Therein the taste of first stones, the hands of dead slaves,
Waters men drank in the earliest frightful woods,
Flint chips, and peat, and the cinders of buried camps.

Scrubbed under faucet water the planet skin
Polishes yellow, but tears to the plain insides;
Parching, the white's blue-hearted like hungry hands.

All of the cold dark kitchens, and war-frozen gray
Evening at window; I remember so many
Peeling potatoes quietly into chipt pails.

'It was potatoes saved us, they kept us alive.'
Then they had something to say akin to praise
For the mean earth-apples, too common to cherish or steal.

Times being hard, the Sikh and the Senegalese,
Hobo and Okie, the body of Jesus the Jew,
Vestigial virtues, are eaten; we shall survive.

What has not lost its savor shall hold us up,
And we are praising what saves us, what fills the need.
(Soon there'll be packets again, with Algerian fruits.)

Oh, it will not bear polish, the ancient potato.
Needn't be nourished by Caesars, will blow anywhere,
Hidden by nature, counted-on, stubborn and blind.

You may have noticed the bush that it pushes to air,
Comical-delicate, sometimes with second-rate flowers
Awkward and milky and beautiful only to hunger.

Night of Battle
Europe: 1944
as regarded from a great distance

Impersonal the aim
Where giant movements tend;
Each man appears the same;
Friend vanishes from friend.

In the long path of lead
That changes place like light
No shape of hand or head
Means anything tonight.

Only the common will
For which explosion spoke;
And stiff on field and hill
The dark blood of the folk.

To a Military Rifle, 1942

The times come round again;
The private life is small;
And individual men
Are counted not at all.
Now life is general,
And the bewildered Muse,
Thinking what she has done,
Confronts the daily news.

Blunt emblem, you have won:
With carven stock unbroke,
With core of steel, with crash
Of mass, and fading smoke;
Your fire leaves little ash;
Your balance on the arm
Points whither you intend;
Your bolt is smooth with charm.
When other concepts end,
This concept, hard and pure,
Shapes every mind therefor.
The time is yours, be sure,
Old Hammerheel of War.

I cannot write your praise
When young men go to die;
Nor yet regret the ways
That ended with this hour.
The hour has come. And I,
Who alter nothing, pray
That men, surviving you,
May learn to do and say
The difficult and true,
True shape of death and power.

JUDITH WRIGHT

The Trains

Tunnelling through the night, the trains pass
in a splendour of power, with a sound like thunder
shaking the orchards, waking
the young from a dream, scattering like glass
the old men's sleep; laying
a black trail over the still bloom of the orchards.
The trains go north with guns.

Strange primitive piece of flesh, the heart laid quiet
hearing their cry pierce through its thin-walled cave
recalls the forgotten tiger
and leaps awake in its old panic riot;

and how shall mind be sober,
since blood's red thread still binds us fast in history?
Tiger, you walk through all our past and future,
troubling the children's sleep; laying
a reeking trail across our dream of orchards.

Racing on iron errands, the trains go by,
and over the white acres of our orchards
hurl their wild summoning cry, their animal cry . . .
the trains go north with guns.

EI YAMAGUCHI

The Setting Sun

We press forward
with our bayonets glinting in the setting sun.

Three girls, clasped hand in hand,
sink into the creek.

On the darkling ground
only we are left behind.

*Translated from the Japanese by Ichiro Kônô
and Rikutaro Fukada*

Further Reading

HISTORY

A. J. P. Taylor, *The Second World War: An Illustrated History* (Penguin, 1976)

Joanna Bourke, *The Second World War: A People's History* (OUP, 2001)

John Keegan, *The History of the Second World War* (Random House, 1989)

Alan Ross, *Colours of War: War Art 1939–45* (Jonathan Cape, 1983)

ANTHOLOGIES

Brian Gardner, ed., *The Terrible Rain: The War Poets 1939–45,* (Methuen, 1966)

Desmond Graham, ed., *Poetry of the Second World War: An International Anthology* (Chatto & Windus, 1995)

Simon Featherstone, *War Poetry: An Introductory Reader* (Routledge, 1995)

Paul Fussell, ed., *The Bloody Game: An Anthology of Modern War* (Scribners, 1991)

Charles Hamblett, ed., *I Burn for England: An Anthology of the Poetry of World War II* (Leslie Frewin, 1966)

Ian Hamilton, ed., *The Poetry of War 1939–45* (Alan Ross, 1965)

M. Page, ed., *Songs and Ballads of World War II* (London: Granada, 1975)

Anne Powell, ed., *Shadows of War: British Women's Poetry of the Second World War* (Sutton, 1999)

Catherine Reilly, ed., *Chaos of the Night: Women's Poetry and Verse of the Second World War* (Virago, 1984)

Victor Selwyn, Erik de Mauny, Ian Fletcher, G. S. Fraser, John Waller, eds, with an introduction by Lawrence Durrell, *Return to Oasis: War Poems. Recollections from the Middle East 1940–1946,* (Salamander Oasis Trust, 1980)

Jon Stallworthy, ed., *The Oxford Book of War Poetry* (OUP, 1984)

Victor Selwyn, ed., *The Voice of War: Poems of the Second World War* (Penguin in Association with the Salamander Oasis Trust, 1996)

Daniel Weissbort, ed., *The Poetry of Survival: Post-War Poetry of Central and Eastern Europe* (Anvil, 1991)

Biographical Notes

VALENTINE ACKLAND (1906–69). English: studied at Queen's College, London; published poems with her partner, Sylvia Townsend Warner, 1933; worked as Civil Defence clerk in Dorset during WWII. *The Nature of the Moment* (1973).

ANNA AKHMATOVA (1889–1966). Russian: b. St Petersburg; Acmeist poet; evacuated to Tashkent from Leningrad 1941–4; considered the major Russian poet of her time. *Complete Poems of Anna Akhmatova*, trans. Judith Hemschemeyer (1992).

LOUIS ARAGON (1897–1982). French: with Andre Breton, leading Surrealist poet and novelist; joined Communist Party 1931; served in resistance during WWII, publishing numerous *contrebande* volumes in the Southern zone and *Le Musée Grevin*, an attack on Vichy and Hitler, and *La Diane Française* (1945).

W. H. AUDEN (1907–73). English: b. York; studied at Oxford presiding English poet of the 30s; wrote 'Spain' and served as ambulance driver in Spanish Civil War; *Journey to a War* (1938); emigrated to US 1938, where he spent the war years, arousing vocal criticism in Britain; visited Germany at the end of the war.

SAMUEL BECKETT (1906–89). Irish: b. Dublin; studied at Trinity College; poet, novelist and playwright, who settled in Paris in 1939; during the war he worked for the Resistance, going into hiding in Roussillon after the German occupation of Paris; worked for the Irish Red Cross at Saint-Lô, 1945; Nobel Prize for Literature. *Collected Poems in English and French* (1977).

ELIZABETH BISHOP (1911–79). American: b. Worcester, Massachusetts; studied at Vassar College; a friend of Marianne Moore and Robert Lowell, she became one of the leading poets of her time; 'Roosters', written in Key West and published in *The New Republic* in 1941, emphasises, she said in a letter, 'the essential baseness of militarism', and recalls the 'violent roosters Picasso did in connection with his Guernica picture'. *Complete Poems 1927–79* (1983).

JOHANNES BOBROWSKI (1917–65). German: b. Tilsit; studied art history at Königsberg; served in German army in WWII in Russia; POW in Russia 1945–9; returned to East Berlin. *Shadow Land* (1966).

BERTOLT BRECHT (1891–1956). German: b. Augsburg; Marxist poet and playwright; fled Nazi Germany 1933; worked in exile in Denmark and Finland, before taking refuge in America in 1941; appeared before Un-American Activities Committee in 1947; returned to East Germany and founded Berliner Ensemble 1947. *Svendborger Gedichte* (*Svendborg Poems* 1939); *Poems 1913–1956*, ed. John Willett and Ralph Manheim (1976).

NORMAN CAMERON (1905–53): educated at Oxford; worked for propaganda unit during WWII; *Collected Poems and Selected Translations*, ed. Warren Hope and Jonathan Barker (1990).

DAVID CAMPBELL (1915–79) Australian: b. Adelong; studied at Cambridge; served with distinction in Australian Air Force during WWII; *Speak with the Sun* (1949); *Collected Poems* (1989).

JEAN CASSOU (1897–1986). French: a member of one of the first Resistance networks, he was arrested by Vichy police in 1941 and imprisoned; denied writing materials during his imprisonment, he composed and memorised a sequence of sonnets later published by Editions de Minuit as *33 Sonnets Composés en Secret* (1944) by Jean Noir, with a preface by Louis Aragon. *33 Sonnets of the Resistance*, trans. Timothy Adès (2002).

CHARLES CAUSLEY (1917–2003). English: b. Launceston, Cornwall; served in Royal Navy 1940–6; he wrote later that 'the war had a catalytic effect on me as a writer'. *Collected Poems* (1992).

PAUL CELAN (1920–70). Romanian: b. Czernowitz, Bukovina, into a Jewish family; 1942 parents deported; mother shot by Nazis, father died in camp; he spent a period of forced labour in Romanian camps (1942–4); 1944 worked in psychiatric hospital in Bucharest, tending Soviet airmen; fled Soviet Bucharest in 1947; settled in Paris in 1948, where he lived until his suicide in 1970. 'Todesfuge', published in Bucharest (1947) and Germany (1952), became the 'benchmark for poetry "after Auschwitz" ' (John

Felstiner). Paul Celan, *Selected Poems*, translated and introduced Michael Hamburger (London: Penguin, 1990); *Selected Poetry and Prose of Paul Celan*, trans. John Felstiner (2001).

ALICE COATS (1905–78). English: b. Birmingham; studied in Birmingham and Slade Schools of Art; served in Women's Land Army throughout WWII; published in *Poems of the Land Army* (1945).

R. N. CURREY (1907–2001). b. South Africa; joined British army 1941; posted to India 1943; in *This Other Planet* (1945) he 'sought to express (his) sense of exile in this world of machines'; co-editor of *Poems from India*, a forces anthology. Ian Hamilton, ed., *The Poetry of War 1939–1945* (1966).

ROBERT DESNOS (1900–45) French: one of the earliest and most active Surrealist poets; broke with Surrealists, 1930; worked in Resistance group in the war, publishing *contrebande* and clandestine poetry, collected in *Destinée Arbitraire*; arrested by Nazis 1944; died in concentration camp. Ian Higgins, *Anthology of Second World War French Poetry* (1994).

KEITH DOUGLAS (1920–44). English: b. Tunbridge Wells; studied at Oxford, enlisted in September 1939; served in North Africa 1941–3; wounded in action at Wadi Zem Zem; killed in action as tank commander in main assault on Normandy beaches, 1944. *Alamein to Zem Zem* (1979); *Complete Poems*, ed. Desmond Graham (1978).

RICHARD EBERHART (1904–2005). American: b. Austin, Minnesota; aerial gunnery instructor in US Navy, writing 'The Fury of Aerial Bombardment' in Dam Neck, Virginia, where he 'taught tens of thousands of young Americans to shoot the .50 calibre Browning machine gun from aircraft'. *Collected Poems* (1960).

GÜNTER EICH (1907–72). German: fought in German army 1939–45; poet and playwright; Hans Magnus Enzensberger wrote that 'Inventory' was 'the birth certificate of the new German poetry'. *Modern German Poetry*, ed. Michael Hamburger.

T. S. ELIOT (1885–1965). American, naturalised English: b. St Louis; studied at Harvard and Oxford; settled in England in 1914;

The Waste Land (1922) established him as the leading modernist poet of his generation; British citizenship 1927; during WWII he acted as a fire-warden and published *Four Quartets* (1943); Nobel Prize for Literature 1948.

PAUL ÉLUARD (1895–1952). French: one of the first and most successful Surrealist poets; joined Communist Party in 1942; spent most of the Occupation in Paris involved in promoting the Resistance, publishing *contrebande* and clandestine books of poetry. *Au Rendez-vous Allemand* (1944); *Oeuvres Complètes* (1968), volume 1.

ODYSSEUS ELYTIS (1911–96). Greek: b. Heraklion, Crete; studied law at Athens University; *Orientations* (1940); Served as Second Lieutenant in the Greek army on the Albanian front in the Greek–Italian war; *Heroic and Elegiac Song for the Lost Second Lieutenant of the Albanian Campaign* (1946); Nobel Prize 1979. *Collected Poems*, trans. Edmund Keeley and Philip Sherrard (1977).

WILLIAM EMPSON (1906–84). English: b. Yorkshire; studied at Cambridge; *Seven Types of Ambiguity* (1930) and *Poems* (1935) established him as a key critic and poet; taught in Tokyo and Peking, spending two years as a refugee after Japanese invasion of China; worked for BBC in the war. *Gathering Storm* (1940); *The Complete Poems of William Empson*, ed. John Haffenden, 2000.

ROY FISHER (1930–2017). English: b. Birmingham; studied at Birmingham University; American-influenced late modernist poet. *Collected Poems* (1988).

FRANCO FORTINI (1917–95). Italian: b. Florence as Franco Lattes to a Jewish father and Catholic mother; studied law and history of art; adopted his mother's name Fortini 1940; fought in Resistance during WWII, escaping to Switzerland after the Armistice in 1943, joining the partisans of the Valdossa; settled in Milan after the war. *Summer is not all: Selected Poems*, trans. Peter Lawson (1992).

ANDRÉ FRÉNAUD (1907–93). French: POW in Quitzöbel, Germany; after repatriation from POW camp, he joined the Resistance; he became known as a poet through volumes of POW poetry, then *Les Rois Mages* (1943). Ian Higgins, *Anthology of Second World War French Poetry* (1994).

ROY FULLER (1919–90). English: b. Failsworth; entered Royal Navy in 1941, working as a radar mechanic in Ceylon and East Africa, before being posted to the Admiralty. *Collected Poems 1934–1984* (1985).

ROBERT GARIOCH (1909–81). Scottish: b. Edinburgh; studied at Edinburgh University; conscripted in 1941, served in Middle East, captured by Germans after the fall of Tobruk in 1942, spending the rest of WWII as a POW, an experience represented in his long war poem 'The Wire'. *Collected Poems* (1977).

DAVID GASCOYNE (1916–2001). English: starting out in the 30s as an English Surrealist, with *Man's Life is Meat* (1936), a book of poems, and *A Short Survey of Surrealism* (1935); stayed in England during WWII, publishing *Poems 1937–42* and working as an actor. *Collected Poems* 1988).

CHAIM GRADE (1910–82). Lithuanian: b. Vilna to Jewish family; prominent member of experimental writers' group in 30s; Yiddish poet and novelist; refugee in Russia during WWII; after the war published *Your Body in My Hands*, dedicated to his wife killed in the Holocaust; 1948 emigrated to US. Howard Schwartz and Anthony Rudolf, eds, *Voices within the Ark: Modern Jewish Poets* (1980).

LUBA KRUGMAN GURDUS (1914–). Polish American: b. Bialystok, started writing in the Ghetto 1943; emigrated to USA in 1948. She published a memoir, *Death Train* (1978) and *Painful Echoes: Poems of the Holocaust* (1985).

TONY HARRISON (1937–). English: b Leeds; studied Classics at Leeds University. A verse dramatist and film-maker as well as a poet, his early work includes autobiographical sequences about his working-class childhood during and after WWII. During the 1990s he wrote about the wars in Bosnia and Iraq. *Selected Poems* (1995).

H.D. (1886–1961). American: b. Hilda Doolittle, Bethlehem, Pennsylvania; studied at Bryn Mawr; moved to England 1911; after being launched in Pound's *Des Imagistes* (1914), she became a prolific hermetic modernist poet and novelist; *The Walls Do Not Fall*, the first of her Trilogy (1944–6), was written during the Blitz in London; the war also informs *Helen in Egypt* (1961) and *Vale atque Ave*.

ANTHONY HECHT (1923–2004). American: b. New York; studied at Bard; 1944–5 served in US army in Europe and Japan; launched as poet with *A Summoning of Stones* (1954); in *The Hard Hours* (1967) and later books, Glyn Maxwell observes he 'goes further towards confronting the Holocaust than perhaps any other English-language poet'.

HAMISH HENDERSON (1919–2003). Scottish: b. Blairgowrie; studied at Cambridge; in WWII Intelligence officer at Battle of El Alamein and fought in 51st Highland Division in Libya, Tunisia and Sicily; published *Elegies for the Dead in Cyrenaica* (1947), a major poetic sequence about the Desert War; pioneer of revival of Scottish folk music and founder of Scottish Studies.

ZBIGNIEW HERBERT (1924–98). Polish: b. Lvov; began to write during WWII; 1944 studied in Academy of Fine Arts, Cracow, then at Torún; first two books during the Thaw 1956–7. 'Something makes me different from "the War Generation" ', he wrote: 'It seems I came away from the war without accepting the failure of earlier morality.' *Selected Poems*, trans. John and Bogdana Carpenter (1977).

GEOFFREY HILL (1932–2016). English: b. Bromsgrove, Worcestershire; studied at Oxford; taught at Universities of Leeds, Cambridge and Boston: *For the Unfallen* (1958); *Broken Hierarchies: Poems 1952–2012*.

MIROSLAV HOLUB (1923–88). Czech: b. Pilsen; 1942 conscripted as a railway worker; studied medicine at Charles University after the war, becoming an immunologist in 1953; he went on to combine being a leading immunologist and Czechoslovakia's most important poet. *On the Contrary and Other Poems*, translated by Ewald Owers (1984); *The Fly*, trans. Ewald Osers, George Theiner, Ian and Jarmila Milner (1987).

PETER HUCHEL (1903–81). German: b. Berlin; studied in Berlin, Freiburg and Vienna; withdrew his first collection of poems (1932) when Nazis came to power; served in army during WWII; POW in Russia; settled in East Berlin after the war, publishing *Gedichte* (1948) and editing *Sinn und Form* 1949–62; 1971, left East Germany. *Selected Poems* (1974); Michael Hamburger, ed., *German Poetry 1910–75* (1977).

RANDALL JARRELL (1914–65). American: b. Nashville, Tennessee; educated Vanderbilt, moving to teach at Kenyon College and University of Texas; first book *Blood for a Stranger* (1942); joined Army Air Force in 1942, becoming a celestial training navigator in Tucson, Arizona, and publishing poems about his war-time experiences in *Little Friend* (1945) and *Losses* (1948); as literary critic of *The Nation* and in books such as *Poetry and the Age* (1953), he established himself as one of the leading poetry critics of his time; killed in a car accident soon after a suicide attempt. *The Complete Poems* (1969).

MITSUHARU KANEKO (1895–1975). Japanese: initially a symbolist poet, he later became associated with the realist poets led by Kusano Simpei and their journal *Rekitei*, aligning himself with the colloquial poets after the war.

OLGA KATZIN ('Sagittarius') (1896–1987). English: a journalist, married to the actor Hugh Miller, she contributed poems under the name of 'Sagittarius' to the *New Statesman* during WWII; after the war she published *Let the Cowards Flinch* (1947) and *Up the Poll: The Sap's Guide to the General Election* (1950).

SIDNEY KEYES (1922–43). English: studied at Oxford; joined British Army 1942; *The Cruel Solstice* (1943); killed in action in Tunisian campaign. *Collected Poems*, ed., Michael Meyer (1945).

RACHEL KORN (1898–1982): Yiddish poet. b. Galicia, living in Lvov until 1941 when she fled to USSR; emigrated to Canada. *Paper Roses* (1985).

GÜNTER KUNERT (1929–2019) German; b. Berlin; declared unfit to serve in the German army due to part-Jewish descent; after the war, studied commercial art, then became a writer of novels, stories, fables, TV plays and poems. Michael Hamburger, ed., *German Poetry 1910–75* (1977).

STANLEY KUNITZ (1905–2006). American: b. Worcester, Mass; studied at Harvard; *Intellectual Things* (1930); served in WWII; *Passport to the War* (1944). *Poems of Stanley Kunitz* (1979).

PRIMO LEVI (1919–87). Italian; b. Turin into a Jewish family; trained as a chemist in Turin; deported to Buna-Monowitz, a subsidiary of Auschwitz, in 1944; after the war he wrote a series of classic memoirs and studies of the Holocaust including *If This Was a Man* and *The Drowned and the Saved. Collected Poems*, trans. Ruth Feldman and Brian Swann (1988).

ALUN LEWIS (1915–44). Welsh: b Aberdare; studied at Aberystwyth; enlisted in army in 1940, joining South Wales Borderers in 1941; travelled with his regiment to India and Burma, dying in Burma in mysterious circumstances; *Raiders Dawn* (1942). *Selected Poetry and Prose* ed. Ian Hamilton (1966).

C. DAY LEWIS (1904–72) b. Ireland; studied at Oxford; one of the leading 30s poets of the Auden generation; joined Home Guard in 1940 and worked in Ministry of Information 1941–6. *Collected Poems of C. Day Lewis* (1982).

MICHAEL LONGLEY (1939–). Irish. b. Belfast to English parents, studied Classics at Trinity College Dublin, married to the critic Edna Longley. Living between Belfast in N. Ireland and Carrigskeewaun, County Mayo, his lyrics address both natural history and the Troubles and two World Wars.

SORLEY MACLEAN (Somhairle Macgill-Eain) (1911–96) Scottish: b. Raasay to Gaelic-speaking family; studied at Edinburgh; served in North Africa with Seaforth Highlanders in WWII, and wounded three times; leading Gaelic poet of his generation. *From Wood to Ridge: Collected Poems* (1999).

LOUIS MACNEICE (1907–63). Irish: b. Belfast; studied at Oxford; after working as Classics lecturer, he joined the BBC as writer and producer; one of the leading 30s poets, his autobiographical *Autumn Journal* brilliantly captured the moment of the Munich crisis; during WWII he published some of his best work, reporting from the London of the Blitz. *Collected Poems*, ed E. R. Dodds (1966).

DEREK MAHON (1941–2020). Irish: b. Belfast; studied at Trinity College Dublin; thereafter lived in England, the US and Ireland. *Poems 1961–2020* (2021).

JOHN MANIFOLD (1915–85). Australian: b. Melbourne into wealthy farming family; studied at Cambridge; joined Communist Party. *Collected Verse* (1978).

DAVID MARTIN (1915–97). Hungarian/Australian: b. Budapest Ludwig Detsinyi; educated in Germany; 1934 left Germany, spending time in Holland, Israel, Hungary and in Republican army in Spain; 1938 joined his father in London, taking the name David Martin; he published a book of poems in English, *Battlefields and Girls* (1942), and worked as a journalist and in European Service of BBC until 1944; in 1949 he settled in Australia where he became an influential journalist, lecturer, and writer of fiction, poetry, children's books. *Poems of David Martin 1938–58* (1958); *My Strange Friend: An Autobiography* (1991).

LOYS MASSON (1915–69). French: primarily known as poet of the Resistance, he lived in complete secrecy; during the occupation his *Poèmes d'Ici* and *Chroniques de la Grand Nuit* were published in Switzerland during WWII. Ian Higgins, *Anthology of French Second World War Poetry* (1994).

CZESLAW MIŁOSZ (1911–2004). Polish: b. Lithuania; one of the leaders of the Second Vanguard in 30s Poland; under Nazi occupation, edited a clandestine anthology of anti-Nazi poems and wrote *Voices of Poor Men*; his WWII poems were published in *Rescue* (1945); left Poland in 1951, spending 10 years in exile in Paris, where he wrote *The Captive Mind*; since early 1960s, Professor at Berkeley; Nobel Prize for Literature 1980. *The Witness of Poetry* (1983); *Collected Poems 1931–87* (1988).

MARIANNE MOORE (1887–1972). American: b. Kirkwood, Missouri; studied at Bryn Mawr; moved to New York 1918, where she lived first in Greenwich Village and then Brooklyn, establishing herself as a key figure in American modernism. *Poems of Marianne Moore*, ed. Grace Shulman (2003); *Complete Prose*.

EUGENIO MONTALE (1896–1981). Italian: co-founder of *Primo Tempo* (1922), and director of a Florentine library (1929–38); a prominent anti-Fascist, he resigned his library post in 1938, spending the war in Florence but publishing in Switzerland; literary editor of *Corriere della Sera*; Nobel Prize for Literature 1975.

WILLIAM MONTGOMERIE (1904–1994). Scottish: *From Time to Time* (1985).

VLADIMIR NABOKOV (1899–1977). Russian: b. St Petersburg to cosmopolitan family; having published two collections of verse in his teens, he fled Russia with his family in 1919, studying at Cambridge; after time in Berlin and Paris he emigrated to US in 1940; author of a series of important novels in Russian and English, including *Lolita* (1955), he published poems in both Russian and English; he died in Montreux.

ÁGNES NEMES NAGY (1922–91). Hungarian: b. Budapest; studied at University of Budapest; first books *Kettős világban* (In a Double World, 1946); one of the most influential post-war Hungarian poets. *Between: Selected Poems* (1988).

LORINE NIEDECKER (1903–70). American: b. Fort Atkinson, Wisconsin; poet associated with the American Objectivists.

HOWARD NEMEROV (1920–91). American: b. New York City; studied at Harvard; served in Canadian and US Air Forces during WWII; thereafter poet, teacher, critic and university teacher. *Collected Poems of Howard Nemerov* (1977); *War Stories* (1987).

GEORGE OPPEN (1908–84). American: b. Alsace-Lorraine; appeared in *An Objectivists' Anthology* (1932) and published *Discrete Series* (1934); fought in US army in the war; 'Myth of the Blaze' remembers him 'trapped in a fox-hole, slightly injured' for 10 hours or so in the last days of WWII during the Normandy landings (*Selected Letters*, 338). *New Collected Poems* (2003).

DAN PAGIS (1930–86). b. Bukovina (formerly Austria, then Romania, now Russia) into German-speaking Jewish family; during WWII spent 3 years in a Nazi concentration camp; 1946 settled in Israel and learned Hebrew; doctorate from Hebrew University of Jerusalem, where he became Professor of Medieval Hebrew Literature; first book, *The Shadow Dial* (1959); also taught universities in US. *Variable Direction: Selected Poems*, trans. Stephen Mitchell (1989).

BORIS PASTERNAK (1890–1960). Russian: b. Moscow to Jewish parents; poet, translator and novelist, who established himself as a poet during 1917–23 but stopped publishing in 1934 for 9 years; during the war evacuated to Christopol, 500 miles east of Moscow, in 1943 visited the front line; wrote play about military life and poems on war subjects, including 'Fresco Come to Life'; after 1945 neither his poetry nor prose was published but he went on to write *Doctor Zhivago* and numerous Shakespeare translations.

JÁNOS PILINSKY (1921–81). Hungarian: b. Budapest; military service from 1944; POW in Austria and Germany 1945; after the war editor of modernist literary journal and first collection (1946); after Communist takeover of Hungary, silent for over 10 years. 'The war has ended', he wrote, 'and the gates of the concentration camps are shut, but . . . it is precisely this final hush which signifies the supreme reality in our midst today.' *Selected Poems*, trans. Ted Hughes and János Csokits (1976).

FRANCIS PONGE (1899–1988). French: b. Montpellier; militant Communist 1936–46; worked in Resistance during the war, publishing *Le Parti Pris des Choses* (1942); innovative and influential poet, who renovated the French prose poem.

EZRA POUND (1888–1972). American: b. Idaho; studied University of Pennsylvania; left US for Europe in 1908, establishing himself in London, Paris and Rapallo, as a major poet, critic and impresario of modernism; *Draft of XXX Cantos* (1930); during the 30s and the war years a vocal and anti-Semitic supporter of Mussolini; in 1945 imprisoned for 6 months by US forces in Pisa, but found medically unfit to be tried for treason and hospitalised in Washington; *Pisan Cantos* (1948) were composed around his experience of the end of the war. *The Cantos* (1954; 1987).

JACQUES PRÉVERT (1900–77). French: b. Neuilly-sur-Seine; starting out as a Surrealist, he reached a wide audience as a popular, satirical poet with his post-war best-seller *Paroles*, published by Editions de Minuit (1946). As Ferlinghetti said, many of its poems 'grew out of World War II and the Occupation in France, and it is plain that "paroles" means both Words and Passwords'. *Paroles: Selected Poems*, trans. Lawrence Ferlinghetti: (1958).

F. T. PRINCE (1912–2003). South African; b. South Africa; studied in Oxford and Princeton; in WWII served in Army Intelligence; later, Professor of Literature at Southampton. Collected Poems (1992).

SALVATORE QUASIMODO (1901–68). Italian: b. Modica; *Acque e Terre* (1930) was the first of four early hermetic books of poems;

from 1935 Professor of Italian Literature at Milan Conservatoire; during WWII he wrote the more engaged poems of *Giorno dopo Giorno* (Day after Day, 1943–6); Nobel Prize, 1959.

MIKLÓS RADNÓTI (1909–44). Hungarian Jewish: b. Budapest; prominent poet; from 1940 onwards he was in Nazi forced labour battalions; shot on forced march in 1944; when exhumed, a notebook of poems was found in a pocket of his greatcoat. *Forced March: Selected Poems*, trans. Clive Wilmer and George Gömöri (1979); *Camp Notebook*, trans. Francis Jones (2000).

HERBERT READ (1893–1968) English: b. Yorkshire; studied in Leeds; DSO and MC in WWI; *Songs of Chaos* (1915) established him as poet; after the First War he emerged as an important art critic; *The End of a War* (1933), his most important book of poems, was followed by *A World within a War* (1944). *Collected Poems* (1966).

HENRY REED (1914–86). English: b. Birmingham; studied at Birmingham University; joined army in 1941, then worked for Naval Intelligence 1942–5; his poems of the war were published in *A Map of Verona* (1946); he later worked for BBC and at University of Washington, Seattle. *Collected Poems*, ed. Jon Stallworthy (1991).

W. R. RODGERS (1935–69). Northern Irish: studied at Queen's Belfast; Presbyterian minister in Loughgall 1935; first collection *Awake!* (1941); after the war worked at BBC with MacNeice and others. *Collected Poems* (1971); *Selected Poems*, ed. Michael Longley (1993).

ALAN ROSS (1922–2001). English: b. Calcutta; studied at Oxford; 1942–7 served in Royal Navy; his first books, *The Derelict Day* (1947) and *Something of the Sea: Poems 1942–52* (1954), reflect on WWII experiences; editor of *London Magazine* 1961. *Colours of War: War Art 1939–45* (1983).

TADEUSZ RÓŻEWICZ (1921–2014) Polish: b. Radmosko; worked in Polish guerrilla underground during WWII; after the war he studied art history in University of Cracow; prolific and influential poet and playwright. Miłosz wrote that his programatically anti-poetic poetry 'stems from traumatic war experiences'.

Conversations with the Prince and other Poems (1982), ed. and trans. Adam Czerniawski.

NELLY SACHS (1891–1970). German: b. Berlin to wealthy Jewish home and privately educated; first collection published 1921; 1940 escaped to Sweden from Nazi Germany where many of her family were murdered; war-time poetry published after the war, *In den Wohnungen des Todes* (In the Habitations of Death, 1946) and *Sternverdunkelung* (Eclipse, 1949), engaging with Holocaust as well as drawing on Hasidic and biblical literature; joint Nobel Prize 1966.

NOBUYUKI SAGA (1902–1997) Japanese: b. Miyazakik. Hajime Kajima, ed. *The Poetry of Post-War Japan* (1974).

KURT SCHWITTERS (1887–1948). German: b. Hanover; artist, poet, Dadaist and editor of *Merz* (1923–32); poetry books include *Anna Blume* (1922); his work was included in Nazi Degenerate Art Exhibition (1937), the year he fled to Norway; he fled Norway in April 1940 after Nazi occupation, seeking refuge in England; after internment in Isle of Man, he spent 1942–5 in London and moved to the Lake District after the war. Jerome Rothenberg and Pierre Joris, eds, *Kurt Schwitters: poems performance pieces proses plays poetics* (2002).

E. J. SCOVELL (1907–99). English: b. Sheffield; studied at Oxford; during WWII lived in Oxford; *Shadows of Chrysanthemums* (1944); *Collected Poems* (1988).

GEORGE SEFERIS (1900–71). Greek: studied in Athens and Paris; entered Greek diplomatic service in 1926; established himself as major modern voice with *Strophe* (1931) and *Mythistoremos* (1935); after the German occupation of Greece, he followed the Greek government in exile, serving in Crete, South Africa, Egypt, London and Italy; Nobel Prize 1983. *Complete Poems*, trans. by Edmund Keeley and Philip Sherrard (1995).

JAROSLAV SEIFERT (1901–86) Czech: b. Prague; he published his first collection of poems in 1921, becoming a leading representative of the Czech avant-garde and editor of Communist papers; 1930 expelled from Communist Party; during German occupation he was editor of the daily *Narodni Práce*; abandoned journalism in 1949; Nobel Prize 1984. *Selected Poems*, trans. Ewald Osers (1986).

LOUIS SIMPSON (1923–2012). American: b. Jamaica; emigrated to US 1940; studied at Columbia University; 1943–5 served in 101st Airborne Division in France, Holland, Belgium and Germany; returning to Paris in 1948 after a nervous breakdown wrote 'Carentan O Carentan', based on a dream and memory of his first time under fire (Carentan was the site of a battle in the invasion of Normandy in June 1944). Thereafter began 'piecing the war together' in other poems, publishing *The Arrivistes* in France (1949); returned to US to pursue a successful career as poet and critic. Memoir *Air with Armed Men* (1972); *New Collected Poems 1940–2001* (1988).

KENNETH SLESSOR (1901–71). Australian: b. Orange, New South Wales; published 1924; Australian official war correspondent in Greece, Libya, Egypt and New Guinea; *100 Poems* (1944); though he produced a small output over a short span, he is widely held to be Australia's first modern poet. *Selected Poetry and Prose*. To the poem 'An Inscription for Dog River' he appended this note: ' "At this point the hills approach the sea and rise high above the river; together they form a very serious obstacle which had to be negotiated by every army marching along the shore. Here the Egyptian Pharaohs therefore commemorated their successes, and their example was followed by all subsequent conquerors, Assyrian, Babylonian, Roman (and French) down to 1920." – *Steimatzky's Guide to Syria and the Lebanon*. In 1942, General Sir Thomas Blamey had an inscription cut to celebrate the capture of Damour by Australian troops under his command.'

BORIS SLUTSKY (1919–86). Russian: b. Ukraine; studied in Moscow; served in Russian Army 1941–5; his war experiences inflect the poetry of his first book *Pamyat*, which could not appear until 1957; thereafter during the Thaw period he became an influential post-war poet. Daniel Weissbort, ed., *Post-War Russian Poetry* (1974).

SYDNEY GOODSIR SMITH (1915–75). Scottish: b. New Zealand; settling in Edinburgh in the 30s, he established himself as a leading member of MacDiarmid's 'Scottish Renaissance', using Lallans with *Skail Wind* (1940) and *The Wanderer* (1943).

STEVIE SMITH (1902–71) English: b. Hull, but from age 3 lived in Palmers Green, London; in 1930s established herself as novelist (*Novel on Yellow Paper*, 1936) and poet (*A Good Time was Had by All*, 1937); during WWII continued work as secretary in London. *Collected Poems* (1975).

BERNARD SPENCER (1909–63). English: b Madras; studied at Oxford; from 1940 worked for British Council; in Alexandria during WWII; *Aegean Islands and Other Poems* (1946). *Collected Poems* (1981).

FRANZ BAERMANN STEINER (1909–52). German: b. Prague into Jewish family; emigrated to England, where he worked for the Institute of Anthropology in Oxford. Michael Hamburger, ed., *German Poetry 1910–1975* (1977).

WALLACE STEVENS (1879–1955). American: b Reading, Pennsylvania; studied at Harvard; worked as insurance executive throughout his career; he established himself as major American modernist with his first book *Harmonium* (1923); during WWII published *Parts of a World* (1942) and *Esthétique du Mal* (1945). *Collected Poems* (1955).

LEON ZDZISŁAW STROIŃSKI (1921–44). Polish: b. Warsaw; during WWII he studied at the clandestine Warsaw University, worked for the Polish Resistance and published poems and prose poems; died in action in Warsaw Rising. *Okno* (1963); Adam Czerniawski, ed., *The Burning Forest: Modern Polish Poetry* (1988).

ANNA SWIRSZCYNSKA (1900–84). Polish: b. Warsaw; during German occupation worked as a waitress and in the literary underground; *Building the Barricades*, trans. Jan Krynski and Robert Maguire (1979)

HARA TAMIKI (1905–51). Japanese: poet associated with *Rekitei* and *Mita* groups; experienced the Hiroshima bomb at first hand and wrote about it in the novel *Summer Flowers*; committed suicide having being diagnosed with 'atom disease'.

DYLAN THOMAS (1914–53). Welsh: b. Swansea; *Eighteen Poems* (1934), *Twenty Five Poems* (1936) and *The Map of Love* (1939) put him on the map as one of the most compelling poets of his generation; *Deaths and Entrances* (1946), written in the war years, confirmed this. *Poems of Dylan Thomas* (1971).

RUTH TOMALIN (1919–2012). British: b. Co Kilkenny; studied King's College, London; served in Women's Land Army 1941–2; entered journalism in 1938, combining journalism and literature for the rest of her career.

YEVGENY VINOKUROV (1925–93). Russian: b. Bryansk; 1942–5 fought in Russian army, serving on Ukrainian front; the war provided the material of his early poetry. Daniel Weissbort, *Post-War Russian Poetry* (1974).

ALEKSANDER WAT (1900–67). Polish: b. Warsaw into Polish-Jewish family; his first book of poems (1919) aligned him with Futurists and Dadaists; thereafter he published the short stories of *The Unemployed Lucifer* (1927) and edited the Leftist periodical *The Literary Monthly* 1929–32; in 1939, fleeing the Nazis, he was arrested by Soviet troops, and spent 6 years in Russian prisons, including Lubianka; in 1946 he returned to Poland but was unable to publish his second book of poems until the Thaw in 1957; in 1959, he left Poland, living in exile in France, and completing his memoirs. *With the Skin: Poems of Aleksander Wat* edited Czeslaw Miłosz, and Leonard Nathan (1989); *My Century* (1988).

FRANCIS WEBB (1925–73). Australian: b. Adelaide; joined Royal Australian Air Force in WWII, training in Canada as a gunner but never involved in combat; diagnosed schizophrenic in 1949 and hospitalised in England and Australia for most of the rest of his life; despite this, published four collections of poetry. *Cap and Bells: The Poetry of Francis Webb*, ed. Michael Griffith and James A. McGlade (1991)

RICHARD WILBUR (1921–2017). American; b. New York, studied at Amherst and Harvard; began writing in the US army in WWII, where he served in France and Germany; his first book *The Beautiful Changes* (1947) drew on those experiences. *New and Selected Poems* (1988).

YVOR WINTERS (1900–68). American: b. Chicago; studied Chicago and Colorado; beginning as a modernist in the 20s, he aligned himself in the 30s and afterwards with traditional metrics; *In Defence of Reason* (1947) was a major polemic against American modernism, a position consummated in *Collected Poems* (1952).

JUDITH WRIGHT (1915–2000). Australian: b. New South Wales; in England at outbreak of war; first book *The Moving Image* (1946) established her as one of the most influential post-war Australian poets. *Collected Poems* (1970); *A Human Pattern: Selected Poems* (1991).

EI YAMAGUCHI. Japanese: Ichiro Kono and Rikutaro Fukuda, eds., *An Anthology of Modern Japanese Poetry* (1957).

Sources and Acknowledgements

VALENTINE ACKLAND: '7 October 1940' and 'Notes on Life at Home, February 1942' from *The Nature of the Moment* (Chatto & Windus, 1973); ANNA AKHMATOVA: 'In the Fortieth Year' and 'The Wind of War' from *Complete Poems of Anna Akhmatova*, translated by Judith Hemschemeyer (Canongate Books, 2000), reprinted by permission of the publisher; LOUIS ARAGON: 'The Lilacs and the Roses', translated by Louis MacNeice, from *The Collected Poems of Louis MacNeice* (Faber & Faber, 1979), reprinted by permission of David Higham Associates; 'Tapestry of the Great Fear', translated by Malcolm Cowley, from *Aragon: Poet of Resurgent France*, edited by Hannah Josephson and Malcolm Cowley (Pilot Press, 1946); W. H. AUDEN: 'Twelve Songs, I' and 'The Shield of Achilles' from *Collected Shorter Poems 1927–1957* (Faber & Faber, 1966), 'September 1, 1939' from *The English Auden: Poems, Essays & Dramatic Writings, 1927–1957* (Faber & Faber, 1986), from 'New Year Letter' (January 1, 1940) in *Collected Longer Poems* (Faber & Faber, 1968), reprinted by permission of the publisher; DONALD BAIN: 'War Poet', reprinted in *The Terrible Rain: The War Poets 1939–1945*, edited by Brian Gardner (Methuen Publishing Ltd, 1999); SAMUEL BECKETT: 'Saint-Lô' from *Collected Poems* (John Calder, 1984), reprinted by permission of Calder Publications; ELIZABETH BISHOP: 'Roosters' from *The Complete Poems 1927–1979* (Farrar, Straus & Giroux, 1979), © 1979, 1983 by Alice Helen Methfessel; JOHANNES BOBROWSKI: 'North Russian Town' and 'Report', translated by Matthew and Ruth Mead, from *Shadow Lands: Selected Poems* (Anvil Press Poetry, 1984); BERTOLT BRECHT: 'Bad time for poetry', 'This summer's sky', translated by Michael Hamburger, 'The friends', translated by Michael Hamburger, '1940', translated by Sammy McLean, 'Song of a German mother', translated by John Willett, 'War has been given a bad name', translated by John Willett, and 'Epistle to the Augsburgers', translated by Lesley Lendrum, from *Poems 1913–1956*, edited by John Willett and Ralph Manheim (Methuen Publishing Ltd, 1976), reprinted by permission of the publisher; NORMAN CAMERON: 'Green, green is

El Aghir' from *Collected Poems and Selected Translations*, edited by Warren Hope and Jonathan Barker (Anvil Press Poetry, 1990); DAVID CAMPBELL: 'Men in Green' from *Collected Poems* (Angus & Robertson, 1989), reprinted by permission of HarperCollins Publishers Australia; JEAN CASSOU: from 'Sonnets of the Resistance:13' in *Sonnets of the Resistance & Other Poems*, translated by Timothy Adés (Arc Publications, 2002); CHARLES CAUSLEY: 'Conversation in Gibraltar 1943' from *Collected Poems 1951–1975* (Macmillan, 1983), reprinted by permission of David Higham Associates; PAUL CELAN: 'Nearness of Graves', 'Aspen tree' and 'Deathfugue' from *Selected Poetry and Prose of Paul Celan*, translated by Paul Felstiner (W. W. Norton, 2001); ALICE COATS: 'The "Monstrous Regiment" ' from *Poems of the Land Army: An Anthology of Verse by Members of the Women's Land Army*, selected by V. Sackville-West (The Land Girl, 1945); R. N. CURREY: 'Disintegration of Springtime' and 'Unseen Fire' from *This Other Planet* (Routledge, 1945); ROBERT DESNOS: 'Epitaph', translated by Kenneth Rexroth, reprinted in *Anthology of Second World War French Poetry* (University of Glasgow French & German Publications, 1994); 'The Plague', translated by Hugh Haughton, published by permission of the translator; H.D. (HILDA DOOLITTLE): from 'The Walls Do Not Fall' in *Selected Poems* (Carcanet Press, 1989); KEITH DOUGLAS: 'Simplify Me When I'm Dead', 'Dead Men', 'Cairo Jag', 'Desert Flowers', 'Landscape with Figures, 1, 2', 'Vergissmeinnicht', 'Jerusalem' and 'How to Kill' from *The Complete Poems* (Faber & Faber, 2000), reprinted by permission of the publisher; RICHARD EBERHART: 'The Fury of Aerial Bombardment' from *Collected Poems 1930–1976* (Chatto & Windus, 1976); GUNTER EICH: 'Inventory', translated by Michael Hamburger and reprinted by permission of Michael Hamburger, and 'Geometrical Place', translated by Stuart Friebert, from *Modern German Poetry*, edited by Michael Hamburger (MacGibbon & Kee, 1962; 1966); T. S. ELIOT: 'Defence of the Islands', 'A Note on War Poetry' and from 'Little Gidding', from *Collected Poems 1909–1962* (Faber & Faber, 1974), reprinted by permission of the publisher; PAUL ELUARD: 'Courage' and 'In April 1944: Paris Was Still Breathing' from *Selected Poems*, translated by Gilbert Bowen (Calder Publications, 1988); ODYSSEUS ELYTIS: from 'Heroic and Elegiac Song for the Lost Second Lieutenant of the Albanian

Campaign (1945)' from *Selected Poems*, translated by Edmund Keeley and Philip Sherrard (Anvil Press Poetry, 1981); WILLIAM EMPSON: 'Reflection from Rochester' from *The Complete Poems of William Empson*, edited by John Haffenden (Allen Lane/The Penguin Press, 2000), reprinted by permission of Penguin Books Ltd; ROY FISHER: 'The Entertainment of War' from *The Dow Low Drop: New & Selected Poems* (Bloodaxe Books, 1996), reprinted by permission of the publisher; FRANCO FORTINI: 'Italy 1942', 'Marching Orders', '1944–1947' and 'Endlösung' from *Summer is not all: Selected Poems*, translated by Peter Lawson (Carcanet Press, 1992); ANDRE FRENAUD: 'The Magi', translated by Keith Bosley, from *A Round O* by André Frénaud (Interim Press, 1977), © translator, reprinted by permission of Keith Bosley; originally published in *Les Rois-Mages* (1943); ROY FULLER: 'The Middle of a War' and 'Autumn 1942' from *New & Collected Poems, 1934–1984* (Secker & Warburg, 1985), reprinted by permission of John Fuller; ROBERT GARIOCH: '1941' and 'Letter from Italy' from *Complete Poetical Works*, edited by Robin Fulton (Saltire Publications, 1983), reprinted by permission of the publisher; DAVID GASCOYNE: 'Spring MCMXL' and 'Walking at Whitsun' from *Selected Poems* (Enitharmon Press, 1994), reprinted by permission of the publisher; CHAIM GRADE: 'The Miracle', translated by Ruth Whitman, from *An Anthology of Modern Yiddish Poetry*, edited by Ruth Whitman (Wayne State University Press, 1995); LUBA KRUGMAN GURDUS: 'Majdanek' from *Painful Echoes. . . : Poems of the Holocaust from the Diary of Luba Krugman Gurdus* (Talman, 1985); TONY HARRISON: from 'Sonnets for August 1945: The Morning After' from *Selected Poems* (Penguin Books, 1987), reprinted by permission of the author; ANTHONY HECHT: 'The Book of Yolek' from *The Transparent Man* (Oxford University Press, 1991), reprinted by permission of Carcanet Press; HAMISH HENDERSON: 'First Elegy: End of a Campaign', 'Third Elegy: Leaving the City', 'Interlude: Opening of an Offensive' and 'Seventh Elegy: Seven Good Germans' from *Elegies for the Dead in Cyrenaica*, edited by Hamish Henderson (Polygon, 1990), reprinted by permission of the publisher; ZBIGNIEW HERBERT: 'Why the Classics' and 'The Rain' from *Selected Poems*, edited by John and Bogdana Carpenter (Oxford University Press, 1977), reprinted by permission of the publisher;

reprinted by permission of the publisher; W. R. RODGERS: 'Stormy Day' from *Poems*, edited by Michael Longley (The Gallery Press, 1993), reprinted by permission of the publisher; ALAN ROSS: 'Destroyers in the Arctic' from *Something of the Sea: Poems 1942–52* (Derek Verschoyle, 1954), reprinted by permission of Jane Ross; TADEUSZ ROZEWICZ: 'The Survivors', 'The Return', 'Abattoirs', 'Pigtail' and 'Massacre of the Boys', translated by Adam Czerniawski, from *They Came to See a Poet* (Anvil Press Poetry, 1991); NELLY SACHS: 'O the chimneys' and 'Numbers' translated by Michael Roloff, 'O the night of the weeping children!' and 'What secret cravings of the blood' translated by Michael Hamburger, reprinted by permission of Michael Hamburger, from *O the Chimneys* (Farrar, Straus & Giroux, 1967); NOBUZUKI SAGA: 'The Myth of Hiroshima' from *The Poetry of Post-War Japan*, edited by Hajime Kajima (University of Iowa Press, 1975); KURT SCHWITTERS: 'Flight' from *Performance Pieces Proses Plays Poetics by Kurt Schwitters*, edited by Jerome Rothenberg and Pierre Joris (Temple University Press, 1994); E. J. SCOVELL: 'Days Drawing In' and 'Daylight Alert' from *Collected Poems* (Carcanet Press, 1988), reprinted by permission of the publisher; GEORGE SEFERIS: 'Last Stop' from *Collected Poems* (Princeton University Press, 1967); JAROSLAV SEIFERT: 'Never Again', translated by Ewald Osers, from *The Poetry of Jaroslav Seifert*, edited by George Gibian (Catbird Press, 1998), reprinted by permission of Ewald Osers; LOUIS SIMPSON: 'The Battle', 'Carentan O Carentan' and 'A Story about Chicken Soup' from *Collected Poems* (Continuum International Publishers, 1988); KENNETH SLESSOR: 'An Inscription for Dog River' and 'Beach Burial' from *The Collected Poems of Kenneth* Slessor, edited by Dennis Haskell and Geoffrey Dutton (Angus & Robertson, 1994); BORIS SLUTSKY: 'My Friends' from *Post-War Russian Poetry*, edited by Daniel Weissbort (Penguin Books, 1974), reprinted by permission of the translator; STEVIE SMITH: 'Voices against England in the Night', 'The Poets are Silent' and 'I Remember' from *The Collected Poems of Stevie Smith* (Penguin Modern Classics, 1985), reprinted by the Executors of the Estate of James MacGibbon; SYDNEY GOODSIR SMITH: 'El Alamein' and 'The Mither's Lament' from *Collected Poems* (Calder Publications, 1975), reprinted by permission of the publisher; BERNARD SPENCER: 'Salonika June 1940' from *Collected Poems*,

edited by Roger Bowen (Oxford University Press, 1981); FRANZ
BAERMANN STEINER: '8 May 1945', translated by Michael
Hamburger, from *Modern Poetry in Translation*. New Series, No. 2
(1992), reprinted by permission of Michael Hamburger; WALLACE
STEVENS: 'Man and Bottle' and 'Martial Cadenza' from *Collected
Poems* (Faber & Faber, 1984), reprinted by permission of the
publisher; LEON ZDZISLAW STROINSKI: 'Warsaw' from *The
Burning Forest: Modern Polish Poetry*, edited by Adam
Czerniawski (Bloodaxe Books, 1988), reprinted by permission of
the translator; ANNA SWIRSZCYNSKA: 'He was Lucky' and
'Building the Barricade' from *Budowalam barrikade/Building the
Barricade* (Wydanictwo Literackie, 1979), translated by Magnus
Jan Krynski and Robert Maguire, reprinted by permission of
Elizabeth Krynski and Robert Maguire; HAMA TAMIKI: 'In the fire,
a telegraph pole' and 'Glittering fragments' from *The Penguin Book
of Japanese Verse*, translated by Geoffrey Bownas and Anthony
Thwaite (Penguin Books, 1964; 1998), reprinted by permission of
the translators; DYLAN THOMAS: 'Deaths and Entrances' and 'A
Refusal to Mourn the Death, by Fire, of a Child in London' from
Collected Poems, 1934–52 (Dent, 1989), reprinted by permission
of David Higham Associates; RUTH TOMALIN: 'Embroidery, 1940'
from *Threnody for Dormice* (The Fortune Press, 1947), reprinted
by permission of the author; YEVGENY VINOKUROV: 'Objects' and
'Adam' from *Post-War Russian Poetry*, edited by Daniel Weissbort
(Penguin Books, 1974), reprinted by permission of the translator;
ALEKSANDER WAT: 'To a Roman, My Friend', 'To Paul Eluard',
'An Attempt to Describe the last Skirmish of the Second World
War' translated by Czeslaw Milosz and Leonard Nathan, from
With the Skin: Poems of Aleksander Wat (HarperCollins Publishers,
1989); FRANCIS WEBB: 'The Gunner' from *Cap and Bells: The
Poetry of Francis Webb*, edited by Michael Griffith and James A.
McGlade (Angus & Robertson, 1991); RICHARD WILBUR: 'First
Snow in Alsace' and 'Potato' from *Collected Poems, 1943–2004*
(Harcourt, 2004); YVOR WINTERS: 'Night of Battle' and 'To a
Military Rifle, 1942' from *The Selected Poems of Yvor Winters*,
edited by R. L. Barth (Swallow Press/Ohio University Press, 1999),
reprinted by permission of the publisher; JUDITH WRIGHT: 'The
Trains' from *Collected Poems* (Carcanet Press, 1994), reprinted by
permission of the publisher; EI YAMAGUCHI: 'The Setting Sun'

from *An Anthology of Modern Japanese Poetry*, edited by Ichiro Kŏnŏ and Rikutaro Fukada (Kenkysha, 1957).

Index of First Lines

It was my bridal night I remember, 272
It was not dying: everybody died, 128
Kube, Thilo, Mèngele, Gisler, Salmuth, 84
Last night. We went far. In rage, I laughed, I was so mad, 222
Leaves whirl, leaves swirl, 290
Let these memorials of built stone, 67
Living in a wide landscape are the flowers, 58
London Bridge is falling down, Rome's burnt and Babylon, 93
Marvelling at the old masters, 123
Moonlight. Middle of summer. Stench of corpses, 293
MORNING AFTER. Get moving. Cheerio. Be seeing you, 107
My contemporary. He died, not I, 191
My end of Europe was at war. For this, 273
My friends in tanks were burnt, 268
My photograph already looks historic, 88
My son, your shiny boots and, 39
Never a day, never a day passes, 136
Never until the mankind making, 284
Night sky bird's world, 196
No matter how the Soviet tinsel glitters, 190
No no: they definitely were, 200
Not the expression of collective emotion, 68
Now I realise I love you, 83
O, dearlie they deed, 269
O early one morning I walked out like Agag, 165
O look how the loops and balloons of bloom, 235
O months of blossoming, months of transfigurations, 13
O the chimneys, 244
O the night of the weeping children, 245
Of the swaddies, 111
Of those at the table in the café, 177
On almost the incendiary eve, 283
On scrub and sand the dead men wriggle, 59
On the esplanade, 186
On the first day, gazing idly about him, 287
Once more he sees his companions' faces, 148
One does not have to worry if we die, 3
Only this evening I saw again low in the sky, 276
Our general was the greatest and bravest of generals, 266

We have sold our shadow, 65
We in our haste can only see the small components of the scene, 26
We press forward, 300
We sit here, talking of Barea and Lorca, 46
We were afraid as we built the barricade, 280
What are they looking for, 248
What hosts of women everywhere I see, 50
What secret cravings of the blood, 245
What sounds fetched from far the wind carries tonight, 4
When all the women in the transport, 241
When I stand in the center of that man's madness, 142
When my older brother, 116
When our brother fire was having his dog's day, 162
When the daylight Alert has sounded, calling us, 253
When the gunner spoke in his sleep the hut was still, 293
When the man, 140
When they come to bury the epoch, 5
When we were fleeing the burning city, 176
When your forms turned to ashes, 246
Where you have fallen, you stay, 210
While the frozen armies trembled, 167
Whit care I for the leagues o sand, 270
Within the wires of the post, unloading the cans of garbage, 130
Vire will wind in other shadows, 27
Yes, I know, only the happy man, 35
You are still the one with the stone and the sling, 220
You can twist the elastic of your heart, 211
You could go to the Underground's platform, 194
You too, past gentle evenings, are being refined into memory, 224
You who live secure, 145
You would think the fury of aerial bombardment, 63